MUSIC
ON THE
WIND

Meditations and Prayers
based on the life of David

by Eddie Askew

By the same author:

A Silence and A Shouting
Disguises of Love
Many Voices One Voice
No Strange Land
Facing the Storm
Breaking the Rules
Cross Purposes
Slower than Butterflies

Scripture quotations taken from the
HOLY BIBLE, NEW INTERNATIONAL VERSION
© 1973, 1978, 1984 by International Bible Society.
Used by permission.

© The Leprosy Mission International
80 Windmill Road, Brentford
Middlesex TW8 0QH, UK

© Paintings and drawings A. D. (Eddie) Askew

Published 1998
A catalogue record for this book is available from the British Library

ISBN 0 902731 40 8

*To Georgia Grace whose appearance
coincided with the writing of this book
and who has graced our lives with love.*

Paintings and drawings by the author

Foreword

When I heard that Eddie Askew had a new book in mind, I was delighted for his use of imagery has enriched many peoples' lives. I knew that Eddie would not dodge the issues of life if he looked at someone like King David. I also knew that I would get some new psalms for Eddie's writing is often lyrical. In all this I am not disappointed; *Music on the Wind* is a rich source of prayer in the very fullness of life.

We start with 'Dreams' and the need to have 'bright visions of a finer world'. But we are not only to dream dreams but to strive for their fulfilment. We are asked to 'Face Reality' - 'even - especially - when the tide's run out and I am beached in doubt'. Again and again we are asked to direct our gaze to the eternal that is ever in our midst; to shake off the need for role playing and be who we are called to be.

From 'Facing Reality' where would you expect to go but to 'Broken Dreams', broken hopes and broken promises. There is no doubt that we all fail to live up to our ideals and hopes. We need to learn to live with pain, agony and tragedy for they are part of the human lot. But so is the transforming presence and abiding love of God, and we must not let the dark images destroy the reality. Even if we lose our grip of God, He does not lose His hold on us.

This is all very nice, but the desert encroaches and sometimes, like on the day of the crucifixion, it seems there is no answer to our 'why's'. There are times of darkness and of thirsting after God. We need to learn to wait and to trust. Even more we need to discover that 'you'll be there on the road with me'.

In the final movement, because David is human, we are faced with 'full frontal temptation', passion, the fire of God and the healing flame. Every facet of life has been faced, and often full on, and out of this turbulence has come new songs. There is a deeper discovery, 'the tune I play is yours. There all the time if only I had listened'.

Eddie has listened to the *Music on the Wind*. If you listen to what he has heard, you will learn 'to sing and make music to the Lord in your heart'.

Rev Canon David Adam

Holy Island

Contents

Linedrawing illustrations

Introduction

On the desk in front of me lies a small bronze dagger. It's covered in the rich green patina that comes from lying under the ground in the Middle East for about three thousand years before it was excavated. It was fashioned around the time of King David. It has no voice but it speaks to me. As I hold it, my mind reaches out in imagination to the period when David was struggling to survive, sometimes against his own king, Saul, more often against the Iron Age invaders, the Philistines. It is a tangible contact with the past and in a strange way it brings David to life.

This book is not a biography of David. It is an exercise in imagination based on his story. It is selective. Some people may find that I've left out events they believe are important, but in a small book choices have to be made. I had difficulty with the grammar of the book. David was, is, so real and immediate that I kept putting verbs in the present tense as though I was commenting on the story as it happened.

For busy people I have included the basic Bible quotations, but it is well worth taking the time to read the whole of David's story in the First and Second Books of Samuel.

David's story is one of a lifelong encounter with God. Sometimes the music of God's presence comes to David gently like the liquid notes of a shepherd's flute on a soft breeze, soothing and easy to hear. David responds and seeks to capture some of the music in his own.

At other times the breeze turns to storm, the music to symphony, building to the glory of a great crescendo that crashes and reverberates around David, God's presence echoing through every hidden corner of his life, impossible to ignore.

There are silences too. Intervals when God seems to withdraw to the edge of David's life and waits for David to make the first move, the first hesitant step, towards him. No music can be heard, only the sound of stillness stretching out bleakly in the wind drop quiet.

These are the most difficult movements in life but they can become the most productive. They are the *in between times*, the Easter Saturdays, the times of waiting when nothing seems to be happening; but they are seasons of preparation, the pause between death and resurrection, periods of great significance 'At the still point of the turning world' as T. S. Elliot describes them.

On occasion David no longer listens. The clamour of his own desires drowns out the music, turns harmony into discord. But whether he listens or not, God's music plays on, its variations forming and reforming, drawing David nearer, weaving the melody of his life phrase by phrase into the pattern of God's own until David becomes one with the music, and he realises that the music was playing within him all the time.

Eddie Askew

August 1998

Part One

Dreams

Reading : 1 Samuel 16:1 - 13

The Lord said to Samuel, 'How long will you mourn for Saul, since I have rejected him as king over Israel? Fill your horn with oil and be on your way; I am sending you to Jesse of Bethlehem. I have chosen one of his sons to be king.'

But Samuel said, 'How can I go? Saul will hear about it and kill me.'

The Lord said, 'Take a heifer with you and say, "I have come to sacrifice to the Lord." Invite Jesse to the sacrifice, and I will show you what to do. You are to anoint for me the one I indicate.'

Samuel did what the Lord said. When he arrived at Bethlehem, the elders of the town trembled when they met him. They asked, 'Do you come in peace?'

Samuel replied, 'Yes, in peace; I have come to sacrifice to the Lord. Consecrate yourselves and come to the sacrifice with me.' Then he consecrated Jesse and his sons and invited them to the sacrifice.

When they arrived, Samuel saw Eliab and thought, 'Surely the Lord's anointed stands here before the Lord.'

But the Lord said to Samuel, 'Do not consider his appearance or his height, for I have rejected him. The Lord does not look at the things man looks at. Man looks at the outward appearance, but the Lord looks at the heart.'

Then Jesse called Abinadab and made him pass in front of Samuel. But Samuel said, 'The Lord has not chosen this one either.' Jesse then made Shammah pass by, but Samuel said, 'Nor has the Lord chosen this one.' Jesse made seven of his sons pass before Samuel, but Samuel said to him, 'The Lord has not chosen these.' So he asked Jesse, 'Are these all the sons you have?'

'There is still the youngest,' Jesse answered, 'but he is tending the sheep.'

Samuel said, 'Send for him; we will not sit down until he arrives.'

So he sent and had him brought in. He was ruddy, with a fine appearance and handsome features.

Then the Lord said, 'Rise and anoint him; he is the one.'

So Samuel took the horn of oil and anointed him in the presence of his brothers, and from that day on the Spirit of the Lord came upon David in power. Samuel then went to Ramah.

Driving the Sheep

Imagine

Imagine a grassy hillside in Spring. It's warm in the sun and the grass is dotted with flowers, golden yellow, white, and the vivid scarlet of anemones and wild tulips. The hillside is scored by narrow tracks following the contours of the ground, paths worn by generations of sheep grazing over the centuries. Overhead a hawk hovers almost motionless in the blue sky, held on the invisible up-currents of warm air.

Behind us is a scatter of flat-roofed village houses, the poorer ones mud-walled, others substantial in stone. The only sounds we hear are the ordinary sounds of the countryside. The cry of a bird alarmed by the hawk, the distant bleating of sheep. The bark of a dog and the cry of a shepherd muted by distance as he calls to another across the valley.

The smells are country smells too. The odour of sheep and crushed grass; and sweat as we climb the slope in the sun, the breeze gentle on our faces. Just an ordinary day.

Then we hear a new sound. It's music, the liquid sound of a lyre, the notes cascading gently up and down the scale, carried on the soft wind. It's a simple melody, experimental, tentative, changing. We follow the sound around the hillside, and there, with his back to a rock in the shade of a scrubby tree, a young man sits.

He's sturdy, handsome, tanned brown by outdoor life. He wears a simple grey woollen gown, spun from the fleece of the family sheep and coarse woven at home. It's pulled back around his knees, and near his bare feet lies a pair of worn leather sandals. He's David.

We watch him quietly as he plays. His sheep are scattered over the hillside but he can see them. Most anyway. After a few more notes he puts the lyre down, stands up, stretches, and calls to the sheep. They hear his voice, know that he's near.

He picks up a stone, hefts it in his hand to test its weight, then pulls a leather sling from his belt. Eyeing a small bush twenty yards away, he whirls the sling around his head and lets fly. A hit. He tries again, this time aiming at a small rock further away. His sling stone hits accurate and hard, bouncing high with its force.

He sits down and after a few minutes he begins to tap out a rhythm on the ground with his stick, then picks up his lyre again. This time as he begins to play his lips move. We edge nearer to listen. The words aren't very clear at first, but he's singing something about sheep and shepherds.

He repeats it all several times, committing it to memory because he has no paper and anyway he can't read or write. He'll need to polish it before he can share it with anyone else, but it's the beginning of a new song to his God. *The Lord is my shepherd . . .*

Psalm 23

The Lord is my shepherd, I shall not be in want.
He makes me lie down in green pastures,
he leads me beside quiet waters,
he restores my soul.
He guides me in paths of righteousness for his name's sake.
Even though I walk
through the valley of the shadow of death,
I will fear no evil,
for you are with me;
your rod and your staff,
they comfort me.

You prepare a table before me
in the presence of my enemies.
You anoint my head with oil;
my cup overflows.
Surely goodness and love will follow me
all the days of my life,
and I will dwell in the house of the Lord for ever.

Quiet Waters

When he [Samuel] arrived at Bethlehem, the elders of the town trembled when they met him. They asked, 'Do you come in peace?' 1 Samuel 16:4

The writer of *Gentle Jesus, meek and mild* has a lot to answer for. It may be a reassuring image for the crèche, but not for the mature Christian. I've never had much sympathy with the idea that Christians should be professional doormats, constantly giving way and inviting people to walk over them. True, Jesus spoke about turning the other cheek, but he also drove traders from the Temple.

The prophet Samuel is no poodle. Under God he is his own man. Tough, at times even violent. That may be hard to stomach but he was a man of his times, and the times were turbulent. We'd find him hard to live with, but God worked through him as he did through David, and neither of them was allergic to a good battle when it was needed.

Samuel faced hard decisions with courage and, when he needed to, spoke out strongly whatever the consequences. So the elders trembled when he appeared in the town and hoped it would be a peaceful visit. It was, although I doubt if they were able to relax fully until they'd seen him leave.

The crucial issue for me is to know when to be tough and when to give way. I'm not keen on confrontation anyway and, although I recognise its necessity at times, I like to keep it as a last resort. The judgement calls for a lifetime's experience and that often comes too late to help. 'How is it you don't make many mistakes?' asked the young man. 'That's experience,' said the elder. 'How do I get experience?' asked the young man. 'By making mistakes,' came the answer.

Maybe though, one indicator we see in Jesus' life is that when he was angry it was on behalf of other people facing injustice or hypocrisy, and when it was only his own toes that were being trodden on he kept his cool. That seems to be a good pattern to live by.

Do you come in peace, Lord?
I'd like to think so,
but there are times
when you disturb more than you comfort.
Times when you ask for things
I'm not prepared to give
and faced with your demands
I want to run for cover,
hide,
and wait for you to go away.

I tell myself I'm seeking peace
but I've a strong suspicion
that I'm really looking
for a bit of quiet.
And that's a very different thing.

I'd love a place where I could sit,
indulge myself,
and let the world go by.
A chance to turn my back on life
and paint reality
in comfortable colours.
A palatable palette of my own choice.

The trouble is
that when I think
I've got it organised,
I find your elbows digging hard
into the ribs of my complacency,
leaving me sore.
I'd ask a little gentleness from you
but something tells me
that's not what I need.
The occasional prod
is more appropriate,
reminding me that life is meant for living,
and opting out is not an option I can take.

Lord, help me realise
that whatever life may bring today
it comes wrapped up in you.
And that should be enough.

'Consecrate yourselves and come to the sacrifice with me.' 1 Samuel 16:5

Samuel demands that the people prepare themselves for God's service. Looking back in the Old Testament, consecration was about cleanliness, getting ready to enter God's presence by bathing and putting on clean clothes. Maybe there's a gentle echo today in the way some folk still stress the importance of dressing up to go to church. No bad thing, but not an essential.

There's a deeper significance to it though, one which David sang about later, and which must have been developing within his thoughts as his relationship with God grew more perceptive.

> *'Who may ascend the hill of the Lord?*
> *Who may stand in his holy place?*
> *He who has clean hands and a pure heart . . .'* (Psalm 24:3 - 4).

If David were alive today, I hope he would have put in *she* as well as *he*.

The *'clean hands'* seems to me to be the ritual part of it, but it doesn't go far enough. Pontius Pilate tried washing his hands of responsibility for Jesus but it isn't as easy as that. David added something altogether more demanding - *'and a pure heart'*. Throughout his life David had a problem living up to it, and so do we.

We make sporadic efforts but they don't last. Somehow we lose the motivation. It's significant that when we describe a lack of commitment we say 'my heart's not in it'. Someone said, 'Guilt isn't so much about what we do as about what we are'. It's about what goes on inside, something that Samuel emphasises in v. 7 when he reminds them that God looks deeper than we do, gets to the root within us and sees the motives for what we do.

It's the underlying bias that's important. Clean hands is one thing; the pure heart - the resolve to live up to the standards we know are right - is another. But that's what counts. The great thing is that God encourages us to keep on trying however many times we lose our way.

The outward bit's all right, Lord.
I can cope with that.
Clean hands.
As long as you don't probe too deep.
I can impress the casual onlooker.
I've learnt the words
and in all ordinary circumstances
I can strike the attitude
that fits the situation.
The words are there,
although they're just a thin veneer
that hides the underlying weaknesses.
Scratch the surface
and you'll find
a very different picture underneath.

It's not that I don't try.
I do.
But when the pressure comes,
my resolution sickens and grows weak
and, struggle as I may,
the inner tensions rise again.
The pure heart that I strive for
seems in almost constant need
of life support.
A daily case for intensive care
before it reaches terminal decline.

Lord, help me in the fight
that still goes on inside.
And when your hill seems steeper
than I can manage
and I stand gasping, near exhaustion,
give me the strength to start again.
However many times I slip,
take hold
and set me back on to my feet.
Return me to the path
and tell me yet again
I climb the hill with you.

But the Lord said to Samuel, 'Do not consider his appearance or his height, for I have rejected him. The Lord does not look at the things man looks at. Man looks at the outward appearance, but the Lord looks at the heart.' 1 Samuel 16:7

I wonder whether we value motive as much as we should. 'It's results that count,' we say. And certainly the world we live in concentrates on achievement. To be successful is all, to make money, to rise to the top job, to be the person with real influence. And if we don't make the grade, we're thought less of.

The other side of the coin is when we say, 'He meant well.' It usually has an underlying if unacknowledged implication of failure, and is used as a charitable excuse before we turn away. Meaning well doesn't seem to be enough.

Taking motives into account isn't easy. For one thing they can't be seen. They're in those hidden pigeonholes of personality that are hard to open. For another, human motives are often mixed, and our actions come from a jumble of selfish and unselfish attitudes. And if we can't know what's going on in anyone's mind then we need to give them the benefit of the doubt.

But surely what we intend is as important as what we achieve. We can't all reach the heights, but we can be sincere in what we try to do and be given some credit for it. David achieved a lot in his lifetime but a great deal of it was built on the backs of thousands of unknown people who just got on with the smaller things which supported and strengthened what he was led to do.

Samuel needed reminding to look deeper than the outward appearance, however attractive that might seem. And even though David is described later in megastar fashion, that's not why he was chosen. Honest, humble service ought to be valued as the great achievement it is and honoured more.

Even Samuel got it wrong, Lord,
sometimes,
so I'm in good company.
I think.

So eager for your work,
enthusiasm clouding judgement,
he grabbed the first conclusion
that looked him in the face.
Content with what he saw,
the easy answer,
the problem solved,
wrapped up and neatly put away.
Till you stepped in
and told him to dig deeper,
think things through
and wait for you.

Same thing with me.
The instant judgement made -
quicker than coffee in a mug
and just as comforting -
but usually wrong.
Lord, hold me back
until I've time to take a breath.
Time, if I'm pushed,
to pray,
although I don't do that
as often as I might,
and when I do
it's often as a last resort.
Time to look at things and people
with the eye of love,
your eye,
and leave the rest where it belongs.
With you.

'There is still the youngest,' Jesse answered, 'but he is tending the sheep.'
1 Samuel 16:11

Jesse didn't even name his youngest son to Samuel. He was just the shepherd boy out on the hillside, too insignificant to be called to meet the prophet, and the sheep too valuable to be left.

Perhaps that was the way David was treated within the large extended family he was part of. There were eight brothers altogether. We're not told how many sisters, they seem to rate even lower than a younger brother during the patriarchal days in which this story was written down. And with the wives and babies of the older brothers, life must have been pretty crowded.

'Oh, you wouldn't want to see him,' Jesse tells Samuel. Jumping to conclusions can be dangerous and so can second-guessing other people's thoughts. How often I've heard someone say, 'Don't ask her, she wouldn't want to do that', without giving her the chance to speak for herself. Often people in that position do say 'no' because they sense that the enquiry is half-hearted anyway. Allow people the dignity of making up their own minds.

It's part of the respect we need to give to other people, and respect should have no sliding scale depending on age or status. And assessing status is a value judgement that takes us into very tricky territory. Jesus turned these judgements upside-down when he invited a child into the disciples' company.

I wonder if Samuel's heart jumped at Jesse's words. Did he see any significance in David being out tending the sheep? Kings in those days were often described as shepherds of their people. Certainly he wanted David brought quickly. And when David stood before Samuel, the encounter was enough to convince him that David was the one God wanted.

*Lord, I'm thankful
that you've never put me down,
made me feel bad or worthless.*

*I've felt those things
more often than I care to count,
and sometimes deeply.
But when I think about it,
I see the hand of my own guilt at work,
my hand, not yours.
My own creation,
a little monster brought to life,
perversely valued, running wild.
Keeping me distanced
from the love you offer.
You love me, not for any great achievement -
I am no David, Lord, nor even Samuel -
but for myself.
And not for what I might become
but as I am, right now.
It liberates me, Lord,
gives me the freedom
that I need to be myself.*

*I wish I had the grace
to see the world that way.
It's all so easy
putting people into pigeonholes
to sort and label,
young, old, or just plain awkward.
It leaves me feeling comfortable
to know where people stand,
and just a bit superior - nice feeling that -
although it never seems to last.*

*But that's not how you do it, is it, Lord?
Thank God, thank you for that.
For reasons I can't grasp you value me
and ask that maybe
I might do the same for others.
Show them the honour and respect
and, dare I say it, love
that takes them as they are.
Gives them the space to grow,
makes room for them in love
as you've made room for me.*

So Samuel took the horn of oil and anointed him in the presence of his brothers, and from that day on the Spirit of the Lord came upon David in power. 1 Samuel 16:13

It's hard to imagine David's feelings as Samuel anointed him, but it's worth the effort. The youngest son, left out of the ceremonies, was now brought hot and sweating from the sheep on the hillside and swept before the prophet. During the time taken for a quick bath and a change of clothes, David's apprehension and excitement must have grown and reached its highest pitch as he stood facing Samuel.

David was highly intelligent, with a poet's sensitivity to the world around him. He was a skilled musician too and must have wanted more from life than caring for his father's sheep. Walking with them, lying in the shade of a tree, he must have had his teenage dreams. I remember my teenage dreams, although there are some I'd rather forget!

As he practised with his sling maybe David dreamed of becoming a warrior like his older brothers, and being a better one too. As he stood up and brushed the grass stalks from his homespun robe, did he dream of being wealthy, of having fine clothes and employing other people to watch the sheep? And with all those hormones rushing around his arteries any boy would dream of love. Why should David be an exception?

Then he was knocked sideways. Samuel's words brought utter surprise, created turmoil in his mind. This couldn't be true. Never in all his dreams had he thought to be king, yet the solemn anointing had to be taken seriously and would change his life radically.

The story moves me forward more than a thousand years to think again of Mary's feelings after the shepherds had visited her in the cave where Jesus had been born. *'But Mary treasured up all these things and pondered them in her heart.'* (Luke 2:19).

Each of them had to face a challenge that would change their lives completely. 'Why me?' they each must have asked. The working of God's spirit is as great a mystery for us today as it was for them. David couldn't get his mind around it, couldn't begin to understand, and found it hard even to believe that God had a purpose for his life. He just had to hold on to it and wait. And wait. That's hard.

Not in his wildest thoughts
could David have imagined
where you would lead him, Lord.
He had his dreams
of how he'd like to lead his life,
I'm sure of that.
Yearnings for better things,
hopes for a better world.
But dreams are delicate
and quickly bruised
on the sharp corners of reality.
Vulnerable to all the pressures of the day.
Easier to turn to disillusion
and think that dreams don't matter.
Images of adolescence,
innocence to be discarded.

Save me from that.
There's still a place for dreams.
Bright visions of a finer world
where love and mercy reign
and justice is the bottom line
of all our living.
Help me to hold my dreams secure.
To value them as treasure to be used,
not locked away like jewels in a box,
their iridescent beauty
wasted in the dark.

Help me to live my dreams.
To grasp the mystery with joy,
knowing that dreams
and what I call reality
all come from you.
That both are part and parcel
of my life with you.
Your spirit sowing dreams of what could be
and in their germination
enticing me to strive a little more,
to bridge the gap,
bring both together,
dream and reality in you.
Fulfilled.

So Samuel . . . anointed him in the presence of his brothers . . .
1 Samuel 16:13

There's no indication of how his brothers reacted to David's anointing. By the time the events in the next chapter took place we read of their anger towards David and assume their jealousy, but at the moment Samuel chose him their attitude is left without comment.

One can try to imagine it. Certainly they felt a similar surprise to David's, and a growing incredulity. This, their younger brother, the one who was sent out day after day to watch the sheep, to be king? They were older - the brothers not the sheep - stronger, more experienced. Already three of them were soldiers in Saul's army. David could never step into King Saul's shoes, command men, fight Philistines. Or so they thought.

Little did they know. It's often difficult to spot people's potential. I remember the head of a UK recording company admitting ruefully that when the Beatles came to him at the start of their careers he'd turned them down and said they'd never make it. Occasionally someone very bright pops up and you say to yourself, 'She'll go far', but usually identifying people's faults is a lot easier than identifying their possibilities.

In this case God made up Samuel's mind for him. St. Paul's words remind us that God chooses whom he wants and his judgement doesn't always coincide with ours.

'. . . think of what you were when you were called. Not many of you were wise by human standards; not many were influential; not many were of noble birth. But God chose the foolish things of the world to shame the wise; God chose the weak things of the world to shame the strong. He chose the lowly things . . .' (1 Corinthians 1:26 - 28).

And David must have seemed to his brothers to fit that description. But God knew what he was doing.

The way the Bible concentrates on essentials and often ignores the rest can be a bit frustrating. Even the reactions of David's father aren't mentioned, and there's no reference anywhere to his mother. We're not even given her name.

She wouldn't have been included in the ceremonies around the sacrifice. We can only guess at the mixture of pride and apprehension as she was told the details later of what was predicted for her youngest son. Her identity is submerged, another of those described by Paul's words, although her influence in forming David's character must have been vital, as any mother's is. She can't be identified but she isn't forgotten. Not by me anyway.

Not always easy, Lord,
to understand your mind,
to know the way you're thinking
and why things happen as they do.
Perhaps I shouldn't even try
but blind acceptance isn't in my nature,
however hard I struggle to conform.
The questions come unbidden,
uninvited guests who stretch their welcome,
stay too long for comfort,
and leave their cups unwashed.
But after all
my mind's your gift to me.
I'm only trying to use it.

The trouble is I'm often led
to seize the negative.
To see the seeming faults in what you do,
the weaknesses in those you call.
Forgive the arrogance
that makes me criticise so easily,
the ignorance that tempts me
into thinking that I know it all.
Sometimes I sense your smile,
an eyebrow raised in gentle ridicule
at all my posturing.

'Not many wise ...'
Yes, Lord, I know.
And in my better moments -
although they're not as many as I'd like -
I recognise
I'm just as weak and foolish
as I judge the rest to be,
and realise that strength and wisdom
are for you and you alone.

Lord, lead me deeper into understanding,
that I may look at others
through your eyes of love.
And if I can't see much in them that's promising,
help me at least to grant another chance,
a charitable benefit of doubt,
just as you do to me.

Part Two

Facing Reality

David and Goliath

Readings : 1 Samuel 17:16 - 24

For forty days the Philistine came forward every morning and evening and took his stand.

Now Jesse said to his son David, 'Take this ephah of roasted grain and these ten loaves of bread for your brothers and hurry to their camp. Take along these ten cheeses to the commander of their unit. See how your brothers are and bring back some assurance from them. They are with Saul and all the men of Israel in the valley of Elah, fighting against the Philistines.'

Early in the morning David left the flock with a shepherd, loaded up and set out, as Jesse had directed. He reached the camp as the army was going out to its battle positions, shouting the war cry. Israel and the Philistines were drawing up their lines facing each other. David left his things with the keeper of supplies, ran to the battle lines and greeted his brothers. As he was talking with them, Goliath, the Philistine champion from Gath, stepped out from his lines and shouted his usual defiance, and David heard it. When the Israelites saw the man, they ran from him in great fear.

1 Samuel 17:28 - 40

When Eliab, David's oldest brother, heard him speaking with the men, he burned with anger at him and asked, 'Why have you come down here? And with whom did you leave those few sheep in the desert? I know how conceited you are and how wicked your heart is; you came down only to watch the battle.'

'Now what have I done?' said David. 'Can't I even speak?' He then turned away to someone else and brought up the same matter, and the men answered him as before. What David said was overheard and reported to Saul, and Saul sent for him.

David said to Saul, 'Let no one lose heart on account of this Philistine; your servant will go and fight him.'

Saul replied, 'You are not able to go out against this Philistine and fight him; you are only a boy, and he has been a fighting man from his youth.'

But David said to Saul, 'Your servant has been keeping his father's sheep. When a lion or a bear came and carried off a sheep from the flock, I went after it, struck it and rescued the sheep from its mouth. When it turned on me, I seized it by its hair, struck it and killed it . . . The Lord who delivered me from the paw of the lion and the paw of the bear will deliver me from the hand of this Philistine.'

Saul said to David, 'Go, and the Lord be with you.'

Then Saul dressed David in his own tunic. He put a coat of armour on him and a bronze helmet on his head. David fastened on his sword over the tunic and tried walking around, because he was not used to them.

'I cannot go in these,' he said to Saul, 'because I am not used to them.' So he took them off. Then he took his staff in his hand, chose five smooth stones from the stream, put them in the pouch of his shepherd's bag and, with his sling in his hand, approached the Philistine.

1 Samuel 17:48 - 50

As the Philistine moved closer to attack him, David ran quickly towards the battle line to meet him. Reaching into his bag and taking out a stone, he slung it and struck the Philistine on the forehead. The stone sank into his forehead, and he fell face down on the ground.

So David triumphed over the Philistine with a sling and a stone; without a sword in his hand he struck down the Philistine and killed him.

Imagine

Imagine the scene. Crowds of men are scattered over the hillside. Many still sit around the cooking fires, polishing their weapons, restringing and testing their bows. Some move around, finding friends they'll stand with in battle. Then the horns blow and people begin to move forward into rough lines, shouting their war cries.

Down the hill, beyond the forward lookouts, lies the valley with a shallow stream twisting and turning along its rocky bed. It marks the boundary. Then the ground slopes up again towards the Philistines' camp. In the distance they appear small, just a dark moving mass as they too get into formation. Their noise is covered by that of the Israelites, except for one voice, loud and rough, coming from the valley. Goliath is shouting. His language isn't understood by everyone but the aggression is quite clear.

King Saul stands on the upper slopes watching. This impasse has been going on for days and he's worried. So are his commanders. His army won't stay with him for long, their food has to be brought in from a distance, most of them are farmers and they have families to think about. Soon they'll begin to leave, slipping away quietly in the night. Saul needs a solution.

Someone tells him about David. Saul sends for him. Perhaps he recognises David as the young musician at court; maybe he's just grasping at straws, anything that might break the deadlock.

Take some time to imagine yourself into the feelings of three people: Saul, one of his commanders, and then David.

Saul is on edge. This may be just a large skirmish but if he loses it the Philistines could move on to attack Hebron. He's unsure. There have been several proposals for action, all faulty, but this confrontation must be ended. David volunteers to fight. He may be untried but he's an impressive young man. Saul feels some inner compulsion, a conviction he can't identify. Maybe the unexpectedness will give David an advantage. Saul doesn't know why, it seems risky, but before he knows what he's done, he's committed himself.

As a commander you're startled. After all the long and heated arguments in Saul's tent about tactics, here's the king making a key decision on the spur of the moment with no thought, no consultation. You're appalled. It's a colossal gamble. Goliath is a veteran, strong and aggressive. And who is this boy? You remember him vaguely as an occasional court musician. What's he going to do now. Hit Goliath with his harp? It's impossible.

How does David feel? He has an outward show of confidence, but his mouth's dry, his stomach churning as he realises that the king has agreed. Does he begin

The Dead Seas, towards Moab

to wish desperately he hadn't put himself in this position? Few people go into battle without fear. David's imagination races as he pictures himself down in the valley. What will he do when Goliath moves towards him? Bears attacking his sheep are one thing, but he's never killed a man. Will he have the strength and courage to go through with it? Will he even get a chance to strike? He takes several deep breaths, tries to control his thoughts, and reaches out to the God he's felt so close to on the quiet hillsides of Bethlehem. *'Are you still there? Can you help me now?'* he asks.

Now Jesse said to his son David, 'Take this ephah of roasted grain and these ten loaves of bread for your brothers and hurry to the camp.'   *1 Samuel 17:17*

W e're given two accounts of how David progressed to the king's court. One through his music, being recruited to play his lyre to soothe the king (1 Samuel 16:18 - 23). The other was through his killing of Goliath. Both accounts can be reconciled.

David's job as musician gave him a place on the fringes of court life. Being part-time he was able to commute between home and court. This explains how he could be at home and able to take the food to his brothers before the battle. After Goliath's death David was recognised more clearly and *'From that day Saul kept David with him and did not let him return to his father's house.'* (1 Samuel 18:2). From then he had a full-time job.

Life's full of ups and downs. Whenever an experience takes us up to the heights we always seem to come down the other side into the depths. Maybe that means we're just getting back to normal which, by contrast with the high, seems low. If you see what I mean.

David couldn't have found it easy living with the promises that Samuel's anointing had brought. Promises that made David different, that filled his mind with questions about how and when he'd be king. Questions too about why he'd been chosen, and in the quiet moments waves of doubt must have begun to erode his confidence in God's purposes. There were certainly times when he felt isolated as family relationships changed. Change can create friction. It couldn't have been easy for any of them. When one family member's circumstances change, everyone has to adjust. It's no use expecting the one who's changed to go back to being what he was before. Change brings uncertainty.

His father brought David back to earth by asking him to take the bread and cheese to his brothers. What's more ordinary than bread and cheese? David had to get on with life and he did it with a rare humility.

The heights of spiritual experience don't give us permission to opt out of commonplace everyday responsibilities. I hope we accept them gladly and with a new awareness of God's presence and strength. Most of us are not called to be kings but to live faithfully where we are, knowing that God is with us in the workaday world.

David would need that awareness in the years ahead. Waiting for God's time is one of the most difficult lessons to learn and one of the hardest to accept. We want things to happen now. God often seems to have other plans.

*In the rare moments, Lord,
of quiet -
which drop like little miracles
into the agitated waters of my life -
I feel you close to me.
I float in you,
enveloped and at peace.*

*But in the rush of life
the wave-beats drown your voice
and I am left alone,
or so it seems.
The contact's swamped,
the certainties eroded,
and questions,
how and why and when,
all lurking in the shadows of my mind,
take form and threaten.*

*Waiting for you,
not knowing all the details of your plans,
takes all my courage
and what little strength I have.
One moment reassurance lifts me up,
the next I don't know where to go.
Lord, help me catch
the faintest glimmer of your presence,
and when I can't see even that
strengthen my faith,
the faith that knows that you are near,
even - especially -
when the tide's run out
and I am beached in doubt.*

*The sea's still there.
Maybe I'm looking
in the wrong direction.*

'Now what have I done?' said David. 'Can't I even speak?'
1 Samuel 17:29

History is a bit unfair to the Philistines. Call anyone a Philistine today and we imply that they're uncultured, ignorant, even barbarian. Whenever there's a disagreement about art or music it's not long before the word's used to suggest that someone's insensitive and without finer feelings. In Saul's day the Philistines were actually more sophisticated and had a better developed society than the Israelites, including the secret of producing iron. It didn't make them less brutal as soldiers but the Israelites equalled them there.

David had walked the fifteen miles west from Bethlehem and joined the Israelite forces. Morale wasn't too good. Neither side was keen to begin the battle. To do that they would have had to go down the hillside into the valley and then attack up hill. That would've been a hard thing to do with the defenders in a much stronger position. It was a stalemate, except for Goliath's daily provocation.

David looked and listened. Perhaps he was naive, but with the eagerness and bluntness of youth he began to ask awkward questions. He made people uncomfortable. 'How can this man defy the armies of the living God?' he asked, reminding them that God was alive; not just a tribal memory but a living reality.

He got under the skin of those who heard him, particularly his brothers. All their irritation and jealousy erupted into anger. They called him conceited and wicked and tried to put him down by asking sarcastic questions about where he'd left the sheep. David responded as young people the world over respond in their struggle to be accepted as adults. 'Now what have I done? Can't I even speak?' All the hurt and frustration obvious in his reply.

Youth has a habit of asking awkward questions we'd rather not confront. Questions about society's values, our behaviour and assumptions. Questions so challenging that the easy response is annoyance - a polite euphemism for anger - and a 'You don't really understand . . .'. If there's one thing young people are good at it's smelling out hypocrisy. That's one reason why they're difficult to live with.

Another may be that they make me ask David's question of myself. Am I simply living with a memory of God or is he still a living reality for me? It's a question I'm not always ready to face.

Misunderstood.
I know the feeling, Lord.
Words taken in a way I never meant.
Wrenched out of context,
warped out of true -
deliberately or accidentally,
I don't know which -
with all my explanations shrugged aside.

The trouble is
I've done the same to others.
Taken a word or comment
far too personally.
Given it a meaning
that was never meant,
and in response hit out,
bruising the truth,
leaving the speaker
with a hurt he didn't need,
much less deserved.

Lord, help me hear your purposes
in others' words.
Graft onto me the sensitivity I need
and let it grow and blossom
into the wisdom that accepts
that just occasionally -
humility's blue moon! -
I may be wrong.
Help me to see there's just a chance
the words that make me feel uncomfortable
and, let's be honest, angry,
are true and just.
That questions asked
which point with compass accuracy
to some deficiency in me
may have their origin in you.
And as I face myself
with less pretence than usual,
help me to make the changes
that will shape me
just a little more
into the likeness of your son.

'I cannot go in these,' he said to Saul, 'because I am not used to them.' 1
Samuel 17:39

Saul attempted to dress David in his armour. The image that comes to mind is almost slapstick comedy with David nearly engulfed in a tunic and helmet far too big for him. Saul himself was a big man. Maybe not Goliath's size but we're told that Saul was '. . . *without equal among the Israelites - a head taller than any of the others.*' (1 Samuel 9:2).

The king's armour would have been too heavy and restricting. A tunic down to mid thigh and covered in overlapping bronze plates, a helmet slipping over David's eyes, a sword long enough for David to trip over as he tried to walk. And David the shepherd boy would hardly have been skilled in the use of the sword. I'd rather not visualise the looks on the commanders' faces as they watched the charade. Goliath might have died laughing but not otherwise.

'It's no good,' said David, 'it's not me.'

Saul was trying to make David into something different; recreate him in his own image. Trying to force David into a mould he wasn't suited for, turning him into a conventional warrior when something different was needed. David would have none of it.

But we do it all the time and have it done to us. 'This is the way a Christian should act,' we say or, 'You can't do that.' We try to dress people with our own expectations, from the best of motives but without respect for personality. We even submit to other people's rules ourselves. Its result is to restrict the joy and freedom Christ offers us. In the end, although it's meant to protect us, all it does is weigh us down and hold us back.

Letting people be themselves seems to be something we're not very good at. We find it easier to give them a set of rules. I remember years ago as a young Christian worker in India trying to live up to an image of what I ought to be and do which had been grafted onto me by other people. It wasn't comfortable and it didn't work because it was a pretence. Eventually I realised that the only way to be real was to be myself, and that was how God accepted me anyway. There was no need to be anyone else, no need to play a role or to be a hero, saint or martyr. I could shrug off all the ill-fitting clothing others had suggested I should wear and simply live as me for the one '*whose service is perfect freedom*', as the Book of Common Prayer puts it. It was such a relief.

Lord, the clothes that other people
want to make me wear
don't fit.
I've tried them on,
buttoned and zipped,
stood at the mirror of approval
and twirled in all directions.
I've tried so hard to wear them in,
get used to them,
and still it doesn't work.

And now I've given up.

Not easy, Lord,
to take them off.
And stepping out of them
has left me feeling naked.
Exposed.
It's taken all my courage
to face the occasions
when, in innocence,
if that's the word,
and if I've any left,
I thought you wanted me to be like that.
To fit the pattern
and pretend the pattern fitted me.
But lies are not for living
however good the cause may seem,
and now I've reached the point of knowing,
with your help,
that all that matters
is the honesty to be myself.
Not in rebellion
but in knowing that
whatever others think of me
the judgement that I value most
is yours.
And that's a judgement that I know
clothes me in love
and accepts me for myself.

So he took them off.   1 Samuel 17:39

It's not always easy taking off the armour we wear, because it's not always other people who insist that we wear it. There're times when we're only too happy to put on armour for our own protection.

We armour ourselves against other people. We put on a front of self-sufficiency because we don't want them to invade our space, don't want to be disturbed, and instead of welcoming others we shelter behind the barriers we erect. Sometimes we're scared of showing our real feelings because we might be laughed at or hurt or rejected. So we live a pretence, wearing our armour and hiding behind the roles we play, the masks we wear.

And we armour ourselves against ourselves. It takes courage to look at what we really are, and face it honestly and openly, because it isn't always very nice. We feel it's better to let it lie undisturbed, sleeping dogs and all that, but we can only expect God to help us deal with it when we open ourselves up and take the armour off.

That's another thing - we hide behind our armour from God. All that goodness and holiness, that all consuming love is more than we can cope with. We're frightened to get in too deeply, and struggle to shield ourselves from him.

Whatever the reason we have for wearing our armour, taking it off makes us vulnerable, but it also makes us free. When David took off Saul's armour he found he was better able to fight the battle ahead of him. He may have been unprotected but he wasn't defenceless. God was with him.

You're on the edge, Lord, of my world,
not in the centre as you should be.
I'd like you there with me,
but I'm not ready yet
to open up and let you in.
Your foot is in the door,
that's fine.
I feel I'm in control,
can open it, or close it
as I choose.
But more than that seems dangerous.
I build defences.
Stay close-bound
inside a hard defensive shell
of spurious security.
And lobster-like,
close carapaced within my fear,
wave warning claws
against your loving hands.

Not only you, Lord,
distanced by my doubt.
I hide from others too.
Show only what I think they want to see
and grudgingly at that.
Can't find the openness
to share the truth with them.

And when I change direction,
look inside,
it's me I'm hiding from as well.

Lord, keep on knocking,
and let the probing fingers of your love
open the door a little more.
There's just a chance,
one day,
I'll really let you in
and find the will
to show myself to you,
to them and even to myself
just as I am.
Accept the freedom that you give
to be myself
and build on it with you.

Then he took his staff in his hand, chose five smooth stones from the stream, put them in the pouch of his shepherd's bag and, with his sling in his hand, approached the Philistine. 1 Samuel 17:40

From the height of the hill where David stood looking down, I imagine Goliath didn't look so big. I remember a story of an African bushman on his first flight in an aeroplane. Looking down on the open grassland, he was told that the black dots below were elephants. 'No, they must be ants,' he replied, 'they're not big enough for elephants.'

Perspective does that sort of thing, but as David moved down into the valley appearances changed. Goliath seemed to get bigger and bigger. He loomed large, threatening, dwarfing everyone and everything.

David was living out an experience common to most of us. From the mountain top, when we're on a high, everything seems fine and manageable, but when we sink down to the depths of the valley, pressures mount. The further down we go the bigger the giants seem, the more threatening the dangers.

As faith is tried and doubts grow we create our own giants. Goliath was real enough to David, and so are some of the problems we face. But others are imaginary, born out of our insecurity, although the imaginary giants are still real to those who suffer them. They all have to be dealt with.

All the time I've been thinking about taking off our armour in order to become real people, another thought's been niggling away. What about the call to *'Put on the full armour of God . . .'?* (Ephesians 6:11). There's no contradiction. If you read a bit further the armour is described - the belt of truth, the breastplate of righteousness, the shield of faith. And it's only as we work with God to peel away the layers of self-deception and fear that stunt our growth that we can stand in his strength rather than our own.

I have my own Goliaths, Lord.
Problems and people
looming large,
their shadows
darkly cast across my path.
Some creep up quietly,
lying in wait to overwhelm.
Others stand high and threatening
and I'm afraid.

It wasn't always so.
Up on the mountain top with you
I felt secure.
Could conquer anything from there.
'Your strength sufficient ...' and all that -
I'm sure you know the quote.
But as I face reality
the problems seem to grow
like Alice in a worried Wonderland,
and confidence diminishes
the deeper I descend.
My weapons seem so small and weak
against the titans in the valley.

Strengthen my arm.
Help me dispel the self-created giants
in my mind,
imaginary ogres living on my fears.
And when the ones I face
are real,
remind me in the depths
that you are there,
offering an armour
I can wear in confidence.
And in a love that frees me
from anxiety
I can step out in faith.
And win.

As the Philistine moved closer to attack him, David ran quickly towards the battle line to meet him.   1 Samuel 17:48

T here's a time for prayer and a time for action, although many would say that prayer is action - just a different sort, and one that keeps us closer to God's purposes

David moved down the hill and as he went I'm sure he was praying. Nothing flowery or profound, just a simple 'Lord help me' kind of prayer. The prayer we all pray instinctively whenever we have problems. I say instinctively because people with no articulate belief, no habit of regular worship or church going, pray it when trouble threatens. It suggests that religious experience is deeper and more widespread than we sometimes think and that we all share a feeling that there's more to life than we can see or measure.

Then came the time for action. David picked his stones from the stream bed, chose them with care. I used to view this part of the story with some scepticism, wondering how a strong man could be stunned, let alone killed, by a small stone. Then on one of many visits to the British Museum in London I saw on display a group of sling stones dug up in Israel by archaeologists. They were as big as cricket balls - the stones, not the archaeologists - and trials have shown that thrown by an expert a stone like these can travel at a hundred miles an hour. That makes the situation real.

As David stood up on the edge of the stream, hefting a stone in his hand, I see him looking at Goliath. I imagine his first thought - 'Gosh, he's big!' Then his second thought - 'He's so big I can't miss!' And he doesn't. The disadvantage turned to advantage by the young shepherd who's prepared to take risks for God.

Refusing to wear other people's armour, unwilling to play the role others expected of him, David was true to himself, strengthened by an unreasonable faith that God would help him. And using his own skills he triumphs.

Faith is unreasonable, it has to be. If we believed that only the possible was possible, there'd be no point to faith. And yet, unreasonable though it may seem, faith makes things happen again and again.

Lord, give me the wisdom
to know just when to pray
and when to act.
It's all too easy to confuse
the two.

To curl up
piously to pray
and leave the work to others.
Tempting at times
to lean on you
to such a point
I never see the need
to make decisions,
and call the accidental happenings
around my life's periphery
your will.

And sometimes
in the heat of life,
its stress and busyness,
so much to do,
so little time to do it in,
the opposite is true.
And drowning in my diary
I lose touch with you.

Yet that's the time I need
the stabilising ballast of your presence
to hold me to my course,
steady
in any storm that comes.
It's hard to get the balance right,
to pray myself to action
and to hold you there,
a presence in the tempest
who will bring me through
to journey's end.

Part Three

Broken Dreams

Open Spaces

Readings : 1 Samuel 18:1 - 9

After David had finished talking with Saul, Jonathan became one in spirit with David, and he loved him as himself. From that day Saul kept David with him and did not let him return to his father's house. And Jonathan made a covenant with David because he loved him as himself. Jonathan took off the robe he was wearing and gave it to David, along with his tunic, and even his sword, his bow and his belt.

Whatever Saul sent him to do, David did it so successfully that Saul gave him a high rank in the army. This pleased all the people, and Saul's officers as well.

When the men were returning home after David had killed the Philistine, the women came out from all the towns of Israel to meet King Saul with singing and dancing, with joyful songs and with tambourines and lutes. As they danced, they sang:

'Saul has slain his thousands, and David his tens of thousands.'

Saul was very angry; this refrain galled him. 'They have credited David with tens of thousands,' he thought, 'but me with only thousands. What more can he get but the kingdom?' And from that time on Saul kept a jealous eye on David . . .

1 Samuel 18:20 - 21

Now Saul's daughter Michal was in love with David, and when they told Saul about it, he was pleased. 'I will give her to him,' he thought, 'so that she may be a snare to him and so that the hand of the Philistines may be against him.'

1 Samuel 19:9 - 10

But an evil spirit from the Lord came upon Saul as he was sitting in his house with his spear in his hand. While David was playing the harp, Saul tried to pin him to the wall with his spear, but David eluded him as Saul drove the spear into the wall. That night David made good his escape.

Imagine

Things don't happen all at once. Sometimes the Bible compresses stories with little indication of the time-scale. We don't know whether these events took place over weeks or months, although months seems more likely.

Imagine David's feelings and thoughts over this next period. Everything is going well for him. His dreams are coming true. His friendship with Jonathan is very important to him, not simply because Jonathan is the crown prince but because a genuinely warm relationship is growing between them. How did David feel as Jonathan gave him valuable and significant gifts, his own robes, his own weapons? Feel the softness of the cloth. Tighten the leather belt around your waist and feel the weight and hardness of the sword.

David begins to feel more confident as his experience grows of commanding soldiers in battle. Michal, the king's daughter, has fallen in love with him. What more could he ask?

But slowly the atmosphere begins to change. A man with his sensitivity as a poet and musician is surely aware of this. Saul is less friendly, not so open or welcoming. David catches Saul staring at him from time to time. The relationship begins to cool. His opinion isn't asked for so often. He's accused and blamed for things he hasn't done. David is bewildered. 'What's got into him?' David wonders, 'What have I done?'

Then comes the crisis. David is playing his harp. Saul is restless, that's why David is playing, but the music doesn't soothe Saul any more. It's become an irritant. Saul stands up, agitated. He moves to the wall, takes down a javelin, balances it in his hand. 'Why has he done that?' David is alert, his muscles tense even while he continues to pluck the strings.

Then with a sudden lunge Saul throws the spear hard and fast. Remember Saul is a warrior too. But David moves quickly - he's learnt that in the desperate hand to hand fighting he's been in - and as his harp skids across the floor, the javelin narrowly misses and finishes quivering in the woodwork of the wall behind him. There's a shout of rage and anguish from Saul as he staggers to the door, leaving David's dreams, if not David himself, pinned to the wall.

Shadowed Valley

Jonathan took off the robe he was wearing and gave it to David, along with his tunic, and even his sword, his bow and his belt.   1 Samuel 18:4

Davidʼs dreams seemed to be working out although there must have been times when he found it hard to believe that what was happening was real. Heʼd come a long way in a short time, from watching sheep on a Bethlehem hillside to living in the kingʼs palace.

His clothes no longer smelled of sheep, there were no worn patches or grass stains on them any more. He was wearing clothes given to him by the kingʼs son, Jonathan, along with the sword and the bow. This was a great honour and we donʼt hear of Davidʼs sling again.

Jonathan moved in and out of Davidʼs life as a true friend. At times he was torn by conflicting loyalties, supporting and defending David yet staying with his father, trying to mediate and finally dying with Saul.

The emphasis on clothes intrigues me. Earlier David had refused to wear Saulʼs armour, rejecting the attempt to put him into clothes that didnʼt fit him. Now though he accepts a rich robe and tunic from Jonathan. Why the change? I believe that the difference was that these were given as a sign of friendship, gifts offered in love. Jonathan appeared to attach no demands to them, made no unreasonable expectations. Thatʼs the way love works.

Love accepts us for what we are, makes no threatening demands for change, simply supports and encourages. Friendships flourish where thereʼs acceptance and founder when we try to remould people. Jonathan accepted David unconditionally, the way God through Jesus accepts us.

Thatʼs not to say we stay the same throughout a relationship. Friendships develop and progress. The important thing about our relationship with God is that he welcomes us as we are but then encourages the relationship to deepen as we are ready for it. David came to learn that slowly, and sang about it later. *ʻYou turned my wailing into dancing; you removed my sackcloth and clothed me with joy.ʼ* (Psalm 30:11).

Love accepts.
Lord, I try to get my mind round that
but stretch it how I may
I can't embrace the world of meaning that it holds.
Your love accepts me as I am.
Not to transform me into someone else
or something different,
and not for anything I've done.
Nothing to do with who I am
but who you are.
It isn't always easy to take in.
And harder to accept.

And still I find myself at times
trying to earn your love.
Make myself worthy,
offer you some quid pro quo -
I'm sure you know the Latin, Lord,
a lot of people seem to think so anyway.
I find it hard to take love as a gift
unmerited,
no strings attached,
just offered out of friendship.

Friendship.
A word devalued in our currency,
its daily market rate
vulnerable to every speculation.
Too weak a word
for what you offer, Lord,
and yet it packages so much.
A Tardis room containing more
than ordinary dimensions can allow
of love and constancy
which overflow,
engulf my life and hold me close.
I thank you for it, Lord.
And for a chance
to lose the guilt
that says I'll never measure up
to what you want.
When all you want, in fact, is me.
Your love will do the rest.

And from that time on Saul kept a jealous eye on David.
1 Samuel 18:9

Saul should have been grateful both to God and David. His decision to allow David to fight Goliath had been the right one. The giant was dead, and the imminent threat of a Philistine attack checked. Now they were able to return to their people in triumph.

But the presence of David, the young attractive hero, was giving a new focus to the people's attention. Saul wasn't happy. We don't know at what point he heard of Samuel's prediction for David's future, but whether he knew it or not at this time Saul could accept no one taking any credit from him. He wanted it all.

The singing, dancing crowd of women must have been impressive. The enthusiasm and noise, the sheer excitement of their reception should have been enough for anyone, but their compliments rankled. *'David has slain his tens of thousands'*? The words weren't meant to be taken literally. This was poetry, the sort of exaggeration we hear in opera or pop song, depending on which we enjoy most. But Saul interpreted it too personally.

He was still king but his insecurity was fertile ground for the seeds of jealousy beginning to germinate and root deep within him. He took no joy in David's success, seeing everything in the most negative way he could. The bottle was always half-empty, never half-full.

That's the trouble with insecurity, it can't build, only destroy. Saul was in a hole and digging it deeper, his personality shrivelling as he began his unpredictable slide into paranoia. If only he could have paused, taken a deep breath and counted his blessings. He was king, his people safe, and he'd found a new young warrior who could make him stronger. Counting blessings is more productive than holding on to hurts.

Easy to say, Lord,
'Count your blessings'.
And on a good day,
when Spring is in the air,
horizon sunshine clear,
and everything's gone right,
my spirit wakes,
stretches its arms to joy.
It's easy then.
The alleluias tumble out of me so fast
my feet trip over them.

But come the day
when cold winds blow
and things go wrong,
relationships and circumstances
warp and dislocate,
they soon outweigh the good.
And in the winter of my discontent
- to steal a phrase -
there seems much less to count.
The balance changes
and the joy's subdued,
shadowed by cloud.
Have patience with me, Lord.
And blame ingratitude on indigestion.
Something I ate.

Help me repaint the landscape
of my life in light.
Mix me warm colours
to replace the dark.
Remind me gently,
gently, Lord - I feel a little fragile -
that all's not lost.
There's still a sun behind the clouds
and seen or unseen
your love remains
and that's a blessing
I can count on
all the time.

The next day an evil spirit from God came forcefully upon Saul.
1 Samuel 18:10

T his part of the story leaves me with a problem. *'An evil spirit from God'?* It's described that way twice, in this verse and in chapter 19:9, so we can't just ignore it. But to be honest, I don't believe it, can't believe it.

God is good, the whole emphasis of the Bible tells us that. *'God is light; in him there is no darkness at all'* as John's first letter puts it. That's not simply talking about the level of illumination. Light stands for all that's holy and good and true. Darkness is the opposite and, while it may have been entering Saul's personality, I don't believe it came from God.

Think of the songs David sang. 'I trust in God's unfailing love for ever and ever . . . in your name I will hope, for your name is good.' (Psalm 52:8 - 9). There's another recorded in 2 Samuel 22:29, 'You are my lamp, O Lord; the Lord turns my darkness into light.' It comes again in Psalm 18:28, with the words changed slightly, 'You, O Lord, keep my lamp burning', encouraging us with the knowledge that it's a continuous process. Perhaps Saul's trouble was that he couldn't hold himself open to the oxygen of God's presence that would keep the flame alive. See how soon a candle snuffer quenches the flame.

In the time when this history of God's people was written down it was believed that God controlled everything directly. They assumed everything came from him - illness, calamity, famine. And the only way they could make sense of Saul's predicament was to put the responsibility onto God. From our perspective we'd put it differently, a perspective illuminated more brightly by the revelation in Jesus of a loving and compassionate God.

There's still a place for judgement but we bring that on ourselves by smothering the light and warmth his presence offers. Saul turned his back on the Lord. It's no use blaming God for what we bring on ourselves. The responsibility lies with us.

You take a lot of blame, Lord,
for things you haven't done.
Must try your patience,
or would do if it wasn't infinite.
Thank God, thank you
for that.

It's all so easy,
faced with tragedy
and all the lesser happenings in life
that we find hard to live with,
to point accusing fingers
and heap responsibility on you.
An act of God, we say
and turn away,
the puzzle solved,
no blame attached to us.
Content to think that you
could blight the beauty of creation -
your creation, Lord -
with pain.

Agony there is,
and was,
a garden full of it,
the seeds of suffering
sown by human failing,
not by you.
Your role to take the hurt
upon yourself
and through the alchemy of love
transmute it into hope
greater than gold.
Your presence in the pain,
a promise of new life.
And though we turn away from you,
you wait at every corner
offering
in loving patience yet again
a chance of restoration.

The choice is mine.

. . . the Lord was with David but had left Saul.   1 Samuel 18:12

Some people will be better able than I am to imagine the black despair that was weighing Saul down, tearing his personality apart. The writer describes it as the Lord leaving Saul. That was the way it seemed, and the way it seems to people who suffer similarly today. 'God's turned his back on me. I'm alone.'

It's not so, I'm sure of that. God isn't in the business of rejection. There's nothing we can ever do to stop God loving us. His arms are always open, his door never shut, unless we shut it ourselves. That's what Saul had done, he'd begun to build walls that would keep God out of his life.

It's better understood if we go right back to the time when Samuel anointed David. Samuel's insight was that Saul had been rejected *as king* (1 Samuel 16:1). That's different from his being rejected as a human being. Going back a little further we find the reason. Saul had begun to ignore God's will and make decisions which weren't in keeping with his role as God's chosen king. He'd decided he could go it alone without help from God.

The initiative towards tragedy was Saul's, and God could only wait for Saul's turning back to him. There was no question of punishment either. God is merciful, not vindictive, gracious and not vengeful. There's a helpful definition of mercy and grace:-

'God's mercy lies in not giving us what we deserve. God's grace is giving us what we don't deserve.'

And I'm sure God grieved over Saul as he grieves over each one of us. Like Saul, we may deserve God's disfavour but his love is always available. With him there's always a second chance, but we have to take it.

Lord,
keep me from the pride
that says
I'm self-sufficient
and can live my life alone,
choose my own way
and manage without you.

It's tempting, Lord,
to break the fragile threads
that hold us close together.
They snap so easily,
but if they break
it's at my doing
never yours.
And even though I feel
an urge to stray,
stay near
and hold me close,
your love more prodigal
than I deserve.
Help me to see
that freedom is illusion
without you.
An insubstantial mirage
shimmering before me,
dancing me deeper
into a desert of self-will,
despair the only drink,
and where my hopes
are bleached to bone.

My freedom lies in you.
A lesson I must learn again.
Your arms embrace,
not to control but comfort.
You are the oasis that I seek,
to green my life,
renew its fruit.
And if I ever grieve you
in my inconstancy
then draw me back again.

While David was playing the harp, Saul tried to pin him to the wall with his spear, but David eluded him as Saul drove the spear into the wall. That night David made good his escape.   1 Samuel 19:9 - 10

D reams do sometimes come true, but they're often qualified by the reality of everyday life. There isn't much room for Walter Mitty types who live in a world of fantasy.

David's dreams seemed to be coming true. He'd become part of the king's favoured circle and a recognised leader. The king's daughter Michal had fallen in love with him and they had married. The only problem was his father-in-law. We're not told anything about his mother-in-law so there are no cheap jokes there. Relationships weren't easy. The king's power was absolute in human terms and his word was law, even when it was unlawful.

Struggling to stay loyal, David used his music to comfort and reassure Saul but it didn't work. The crisis came. I hear the thoughts going through David's mind. It seemed strange that Saul would sit in the palace holding his spear. Why would he do that? Weapons had to be cleaned but surely servants would do it. To practise his technique? You don't do that indoors. It put David on edge.

Saul was in a dark mood, brooding, his mind in turmoil. All the feelings of jealousy, anger and alienation were welling up inside him, and in one awful moment of violence his spear pinned all David's dreams to the wall. So quickly done.

It's so easy to throw spears. The angry comments, the barbed remarks we make with no thought of consequences, the sarcasm that shatters confidence and hurts without consideration. It's not always easy to hold the words back. It may be important to let people know how we really feel when we've been hurt but there are better ways of doing it. We're more likely to get a helpful response when we do it with loving kindness as a weapon.

Lord, I remember times
when I've been hurt.
Targeted and pinned down
by criticism.
Motives misunderstood,
often deliberately
or so it seemed,
and I've been left with wounds
that take too long to heal.
And then I find
it's hard to hold my tongue
and count to ten,
though often ten's not quite enough,
a hundred might be better.

And when the hurricane's blown out,
the words that hurt as I've been hurt
all spoken,
I see around my feet
the shredded remnants
of my resolutions to do better.

Then, Lord, forgive
and in your gentle way,
your voice not in the earthquake,
wind or fire,
point me once more
along your path.
Give me the grace,
so undeserved,
to put resentment
in its place.
Not buried deep
below the surface of my life
to sprout again unnoticed
when I least expect it,
but at your feet
where you and I
together
can recycle it as love.

Part Four

The Waiting Game

Oasis at Noon

Readings : 1 Samuel 24:1 - 7

After Saul returned from pursuing the Philistines, he was told, 'David is in the Desert of En Gedi.' So Saul took three thousand chosen men from all Israel and set out to look for David and his men near the Crags of the Wild Goats.

He came to the sheep pens along the way; a cave was there, and Saul went in to relieve himself. David and his men were far back in the cave. The men said, 'This is the day the Lord spoke of when he said to you, "I will give your enemy into your hands for you to deal with as you wish." ' Then David crept up unnoticed and cut off a corner of Saul's robe.

Afterwards, David was conscience-stricken for having cut off a corner of his robe. He said to his men, 'The Lord forbid that I should do such a thing to my master, the Lord's anointed, or lift my hand against him; for he is the anointed of the Lord.' With these words David rebuked his men and did not allow them to attack Saul. And Saul left the cave and went his way.

1 Samuel 31:1 - 4

Now the Philistines fought against Israel; the Israelites fled before them, and many fell slain on Mount Gilboa. The Philistines pressed hard after Saul and his sons, and they killed his sons Jonathan, Abinadab and Malki-Shua. The fighting grew fierce around Saul, and when the archers overtook him, they wounded him critically.

Saul said to his armour-bearer, 'Draw your sword and run me through, or these uncircumcised fellows will come and run me through and abuse me.'

But the armour-bearer was terrified and would not do it; so Saul took his own sword and fell on it.

2 Samuel 1:17 - 19

David took up this lament concerning Saul and his son Jonathan, and ordered that the men of Judah be taught this lament of the bow:

> 'Your glory, O Israel, lies slain on your heights.
> How the mighty have fallen!'

2 Samuel 2:4

Then the men of Judah came to Hebron and there they anointed David king over the house of Judah.

Imagine

Take time to imagine David's feelings as a fugitive. The sudden shock as Saul threatens to kill him. The desolation that comes when he realises that he must abandon everything to save his life - family and friends, Jonathan, his position, even his wife. His world is shattered. Imagine the feeling of unreality, the disbelief, the denial that this could be happening.

Out in the Judean desert life is hard. High stark cliffs throw heavy shadows across jagged rocks. The cliffs are riddled with caves. There are deep valleys strewn with stones and straggling thorn bushes. The days are burning hot with a dry, desiccating heat; the nights cold and long. Here and there you find a small patch of green grass and a few palm trees. An oasis with a well, even a small struggling stream.

David has come to one at En Gedi. It's evening, the sky transformed from burning gold to gentle pink and grey. As the last light fades David and his men sprawl around a small fire in the mouth of the cave they've chosen to shelter them through the night. The air is suddenly chill as the sun dips below the horizon.

David takes his lyre and moves a little way up the hillside, past the lookout who watches for signs of pursuit. They rarely feel safe. David's feelings are as bleak as the ground he walks on. He sits against a rock and as the sky darkens he looks up at the first stars. He plucks a few notes on the harp and begins to sing softly.

> 'Deliver me from my enemies, O God; protect me from those who
> rise up against me.
> Deliver me from evildoers and save me from bloodthirsty men.'
> (Psalm 59:1 - 2).

It's a protest song, and David's anger spills out against his enemies, against his circumstances and, truth to tell, against God. But gradually his mood changes as he finds release from the tension and he reaches out in longing towards God. He can't always understand what's happening to him but he holds on to his faith even when God seems distant.

> 'O God, you are my God, earnestly I seek you;
> my soul thirsts for you, my body longs for you,
> in a dry and weary land where there is no water.'
> (Psalm 63:1).

It's only those who've travelled in the desert and know what real thirst feels like who can truly imagine David's longing.

Judean Desert

Deliver me from my enemies, O God; protect me from those who rise up against me. Psalm 59:1

There must have been times when David's only release came through his music. His life had changed dramatically. He'd fled from Saul into the dubious safety of the desert. His flight mirrored that of Moses centuries earlier running from Egypt's Pharaoh. Like Moses, David was living hand to mouth as a fugitive. Maybe his youthful life as a shepherd had been a kind of preparation but it was still as traumatic an experience as it had been for Moses.

It made David angry and it all spilled out in this psalm. Read the whole of it. It may be part of the Bible but it's not easy to read. There's an uncomfortable vindictiveness in some of the words. There's no doubting how he saw his persecutors and how he wanted them dealt with. He wanted them punished, wanted to gloat over them. He doesn't name them but he'd like to see them suffer as he had. It was very human, if not very edifying.

The reassurance for me is that David couldn't keep it up. Even in his angry attempts to get God to punish, David held on to a conviction that God is a loving God, even though he was trying to limit God's love to himself and withhold it from his enemies.

It also comforts me to realise that there is no psalm beginning 'There is no God.' However great David's sufferings and frustration became, he still held on to his conviction that God was there and was listening.

There's a place for anger, and not just righteous anger. Anger is there, deep down in all of us, and it has to be acknowledged and dealt with. I'm sure God can take with compassion the harshest words we can think of when our distress is real and deep. And even when our anger is directed at God, as I suspect David's was, it's important that we bring it out into the open before him. If we hold the anger down and pretend it's not there, we're living a lie. Going back to an earlier thought, we're wearing clothes that don't fit and it won't do us any good. God's love is unqualified, and far from punishing us for our anger he'll help us deal with it.

I'm only human, Lord, as David was,
although I can't compare myself
to him, and don't.
But I get angry too at times.
Frustration spilling out
when things go wrong.
When difficulties lie in wait
to bring me down.
Ambush my hopes
and leave my good intentions
bleeding on the ground.

And then, Lord, anger erupts.
A lava flow that threatens everything in sight.
An incandescence
surging up from deep inside,
releasing thoughts and feelings
I hardly knew existed
and wish I didn't now.
A violence
that batters down restraining walls
I've taken years to build.

I look around eager to identify
an easy enemy to blame.
A scapegoat I can heap my anguish on.
But when, nearly engulfed,
I call on you for help,
your voice comes through the storm.
Not always bringing peace
but bringing truth.
Offering an understanding that helps me light
the still dark corners of my life,
identify the untamed prisoner within,
who stands reluctant to release the bars
he grasps so tight
of self-inflicted prison.
Resisting to the last
the open door to life and freedom.

Lord, in your mercy deal with me
as once you did with David.
Cradle me in love
and bring me through the valley
to your peace.

After Saul returned from pursuing the Philistines, he was told, 'David is in the Desert of En Gedi.'   1 Samuel 24:1

There was little let up for David and his followers. From the time he fled from Saul they were almost constantly on the move, a band of guerrillas fighting to survive in the wilderness of the Judean desert. Occasionally there was respite. En Gedi was, and still is, a lovely oasis of green around a permanent fresh water supply on the western edge of the Dead Sea.

In David's time it was a farming town. The Song of Songs, which many believe was written by Solomon, David's son, refers to *'the vineyards of En Gedi'* (Song 1:14), a fertile and productive centre of crops and wine. A wonderful place for people who'd had a hard time in the desert. But David couldn't relax in the town. It was too dangerous. He and a small group of his men hid quietly in nearby caves.

They must have known a moment of panic thinking they were trapped as Saul came near, but the tables were turned as Saul entered the cave alone. He was in their power. All it needed was one quick thrust with his sword, the sword Jonathan had given David, but whatever pressures were put on him at that moment, he held back.

There's a time for action but there's also a time for reflection, and David takes it. It must have been tempting. Just one move, one decision, and his problems would've been solved. But that one action, tempting though it must have seemed, was just that - temptation.

The end didn't justify the means, and never does. It can seem so easy to make an immediate decision like that, but if it involves wrongdoing of any sort it can't be right. I don't think God has the word expedient in his vocabulary. Hard though it was, David chose to wait for God's timing.

A time for action
and a time to wait.
My problem, Lord,
is knowing which is which.
Not always easy to decide
when I should act
and when a situation
needs more thought.

Action is tempting.
The macho move
that could resolve
my inconvenience at a stroke
and show me strong and masterful
- the fantasy is nice, Lord,
even though it never seems
to work like that.
I hesitate,
and wonder if it's really strength -
weakness can wear a dubious authority -
or simply an impatience to be done.
An intolerance of things and people
I find hard to live with.
Love works by bringing opposites together
in love's time.
Sometimes it needs a miracle,
but love is more acceptable than hate
to build my life upon.
But in my quiet moments
sometimes I find
more questions than I've answers for.
And in the end I have to leave
my problems and uncertainties with you.
As David did.
Confident - I wish I were -
that all things shall be well at last.

Lord, grace me with your wisdom,
a little is enough for now,
and just a bit of understanding.
Help me to see each situation
with your eyes
and act, when action's needed,
with a sympathy
that can only come from you.

O God, you are my God, earnestly I seek you; my soul thirsts for you, my body longs for you, in a dry and weary land where there is no water . . . Psalm 63:1 - 4

These words come alive when you've travelled in the desert as I have in Ethiopia and Israel. David's words were heartfelt, arising out of real experience. There must have been many bleak moments for him during his years in the wilderness, times when he had to put on a mask of confidence to encourage his followers, even when he felt differently and God seemed far away.

Where was God? Why didn't he help? The questions must have tumbled through David's mind. Occasions when he had to hang on desperately to faith in the promises God had given him, and fight his doubts. The desert days may have been hot but it was cold midwinter in his heart.

You can read the words of this song in different ways. To me the revealing words are *seek, thirst, long*. This wasn't a song of satisfaction, but a cry for help. There's less need to seek or thirst or long for God if you can feel him near. David was reaching out for encouragement, but all he was finding was emptiness and silence. The desert was within, and in later verses of the psalm it seems that all David could do was to hold on to memories of days when he could feel God close.

At times we create a desert for ourselves, turning our backs deliberately on God, but at other times, in spite of all our longings, we hear no answer to our prayers. Our words just seem to disappear into nothing. God seems to have withdrawn. I don't know why. I wish I did. The Desert Fathers, the great saints, all experienced this seeming emptiness. Jesus knew it. Hanging on the cross he shouted a similar question, echoing the psalmist's words, *'My God, my God, why have you forsaken me?'* (Psalm 22:1).

That gives us a clue, because God hadn't abandoned Jesus. Far from it. God was there, suffering with him, and the purpose of the cross was realised. He's there with us too in the silence and the loneliness, and if we question it then we're only doing what Jesus did.

We don't know why it has to be this way. It would be so much easier if God simply jumped in at the instant we asked and made things perfect, but I'm not sure we'd grow into maturity that way. And whether we could bear the full glory of his presence is another question. Children need to move out of the protection of loving parents into what we call the real world - although I'm sure that love is part of the real world - and wise parents encourage them to do so. And as for making everything perfect, I think God's rather expecting us to have a go at that ourselves, with his help of course.

Lord, will I ever understand
those times
when all my cries bounce back
and echo through the empty silences
of life?
When you are far away,
or so it seems,
although I'm told you're always near?
When I reach out my hands
to grasp
and find I hold
nothing more substantial
than the air I breathe?

I scan my life's horizon
endlessly.
Eager to see that first small cloud
grow to a gift,
its promise insubstantial
on the first faint breeze.
Yearning to feel your presence
in the sweet glad smell of rain on wind
falling on the desert of my life.
And whether you come
in dew at dawn gently
or in raging storm
that lifts the roof
and floods each corner of my life,
I'll welcome it.

Meanwhile I wait for answers
but you seem content
to let me find my own,
although they never seem to satisfy.
Yet in the gap between us
the silence stirs,
alive with possibilities
I can't define
and somehow
making wordless promises
that fill the space
and change the stillness
to tranquillity.
I'll wait, Lord.

. . . in a dry and weary land where there is no water. Psalm 63:1

My mother used to try to temper my childish impatience with the words 'If it's worth having, it's worth waiting for.' Waiting is one of the most difficult things we're called on to do. We're impatient. We're an instant people, whether it's coffee or credit, and we want everything now. And to be impatient for spiritual experience is often seen as a virtue.

An American writer, Sue Monk Kidd, observes in her book *When the Heart Waits* that waiting is often thought of as a waste of time. But she says that's far from the truth. Waiting is a time of preparation. She looks at a cocoon spun by a caterpillar and realises that through the winter, when nothing seems to be happening, momentous changes are taking place within the cocoon, and that in time a butterfly will emerge. And to become a butterfly the cocoon can't be avoided.

We need to go through a cocoon stage in life if we are ever to develop further, and that stage in our journey can't be avoided or hurried. Waiting comes whether we wish it or not. Its length is not in our hands and it can happen even while we are apparently living and functioning normally. As it did with David.

David's waiting was in the desert, ours may be in the crowded city, but the experience is essentially the same. We too may become a *'dry and weary land where there is no water.'* And like David we may yearn for it to end, but that's not in our hands. How long we wait is God's decision and he won't be hurried. Rebelling doesn't help. The dry land needs the water but it has no power to make the rain come. That happens when God judges that the time is right.

All the dry land can do is wait. And if God seems far away we may need to hold on desperately to the memory of experiences of other days. The change will come. The cocoon will split eventually and the butterfly will spread its wings in beauty.

The important thing is that in our waiting we are turned in God's direction. Then the waiting will begin the metamorphosis that makes us into what he wants us to be.

Still waiting, Lord,
for that one touch
to open up my life to you.
I treasure moments
when I've felt at ease,
content to wait,
your presence gentle,
intimate and warm.
But now a cold wind blows,
shredding contentment.
Emptiness surrounds me,
draws me into darkness
and I feel alone.
I wait but nothing seems to happen
and time moves on without me.
Or so it seems.

Is there a chance
that you could reassure me
that the waiting's purposeful?
That waiting's never wasted
if it draws me nearer you.
That in the silence
and the dark
your will is working out
its possibilities?
And that the day will come -
soon, Lord, soon -
when shroud will split
and I will burst
the wall of my cocoon
and I'll emerge
into the fullness of your light.
Transformed.
And then
I shall unfurl my wings
and fly.
The chrysalis discarded,
metamorphosis complete,
the promise made reality.

How the mighty have fallen!   2 Samuel 1:19

Jonathan was dead, killed by the Philistines along with two of his brothers. Saul was wounded and surrounded. There seemed no way out and in despair Saul took his own life. A tragic end to a tragic career.

This final act was the climax to years of self-destruction. In all his agony it's fitting that no one else could be blamed for his death. And maybe too it's significant that nowhere in the description of Saul's end is there any suggestion that the hand of God was at work in it. Saul's decline was Saul's responsibility. No one else's. There lies the sadness.

The jealousy and hatred in his heart had blighted his life, corroding and poisoning his personality. Ill feelings, and these were more than that, always damage most the one who shelters them, whatever they may do to anyone else.

It's always sad to hear someone say, 'I'll never forgive him' for some real or imaginary hurt, or even, 'Yes, I can forgive him, but he'll have to make the first move.' It doesn't work that way. Forgiving is an essential part of our spiritual survival, not just our spiritual growth. Resentment sows the seeds of destruction and by holding on to it we kill ourselves by degrees. Strong words but true.

Whatever other people may do to me, whether accidentally or by design, there's little point in waiting for the other person to make a gesture of regret. The only way to break the vicious circle of anger is to do something myself for my own sake. In a sense one could almost say that the act of forgiving is selfish because it does me at least as much good as it does the other person. It releases my mind and allows my energies to be channelled into something more profitable.

Forgiving may seem like a little crucifixion but death on the cross leads to new life. And always did.

Lord, if I should ever seem
to hold resentment dear
and hoard the hurts
that life has brought,
remind me
that I'll hurt myself
more than I'll injure those
who bruise my toes.

And yet surrender can be hard.
Although the bitterness corrodes
and etches deep
into my being,
I still treasure it.
And like a miser
hide it secure and deep,
to take it out
occasionally
to count and gloat.
I'm rich,
if only in resentment.

Lord, break the chains
that hold me to my ills,
that multiply my rancour.
Give me the freedom
to forgive,
to open wide my life
and welcome
those I've fought against
so long and bitterly.
Help me to look
and see in them,
however faint,
your image.
And acknowledge
that you love them,
against the odds,
as you love me.
That way is life.

Then the men of Judah came to Hebron and there they anointed David king over the house of Judah.   2 Samuel 2:4

David had lived ten years in the wilderness, years of danger, struggle and deprivation. There must have been days when he was strongly tempted to give up, when God's promises seemed empty, and there was little satisfaction in carrying on the fight. Times when he wondered whether the promises had come from God in the first place or whether Samuel had made a big mistake. If David had given up, it wouldn't have seemed so much that he was turning his back on God but that God had apparently turned his back on him.

But after the tragedy and sadness of the deaths of Saul and Jonathan came the bitter-sweet moment which ended the years of waiting. David shrugged off the cocoon and emerged into the full light as king of Judah. It would take another seven and a half years for him to unite the whole of Israel and Judah, but this was the first big step.

As the leaders of Judah crowded round David to anoint him, his mind must have gone back to that private family occasion with Samuel which began it all - Samuel's quiet anointing of David and his sharing of God's promises.

The seeming emptiness of those desert years was now echoing with God's purposes and the realisation that he'd been in God's hands all the time. Not that God had willed the years of suffering - they were Saul's creation - but God had been working for good through them all.

Looking back on life we see things with a clarity we're never granted when we try to look into the future.

Lord, sometimes I'd like to see ahead
more clearly.
Dispel the mist
that swirls around the future
and makes my every move
a little problematical.
It would be nice, I feel,
if you could write
the next few steps of my itinerary
in greater detail.
I'd like a timetable reliably constructed,
its routes, departure and arrival times
defined with some precision.
I'm on the bus
and though the seats are reasonably comfortable
I'd like to see the way
more clearly than I do.

But when I think it through -
and that's an effort I don't always make -
I reckon that the reason
that my journey's not defined
is because you give me freedom
to choose the route I take.
Trusting me more, perhaps, than I trust you.
Your hope and expectation
that I'll step out
armed in the confidence
I've found from looking back
and seeing
that in good times and in bad
your presence gave me strength
and comfort.
I don't know what's to come
but that no longer matters
quite so much
as knowing that
whatever it may be
you'll be there
on the road with me.

Part Five

Final Movement

Oasis at En Gedi

Readings : 2 Samuel 11:1 - 5

In the spring, at the time when kings go off to war, David sent Joab out with the king's men and the whole Israelite army. They destroyed the Ammonites and besieged Rabbah. But David remained in Jerusalem.

One evening David got up from his bed and walked around on the roof of the palace. From the roof he saw a woman bathing. The woman was very beautiful, and David sent someone to find out about her. The man said, 'Isn't this Bathsheba, the daughter of Eliam and the wife of Uriah the Hittite?' Then David sent messengers to get her. She came to him, and he slept with her . . . Then she went back home. The woman conceived and sent word to David, saying, 'I am pregnant.'

2 Samuel 11:14 - 17

In the morning David wrote a letter to Joab and sent it with Uriah. In it he wrote, 'Put Uriah in the front line where the fighting is fiercest. Then withdraw from him so that he will be struck down and die.' So while Joab had the city under siege, he put Uriah at a place where he knew the strongest defenders were. When the men of the city came out and fought against Joab, some of the men in David's army fell; moreover, Uriah the Hittite died.

2 Samuel 12:1 - 7

The Lord sent Nathan to David. When he came to him, he said, 'There were two men in a certain town, one rich and the other poor. The rich man had a very large number of sheep and cattle, but the poor man had nothing except one little ewe lamb that he had bought. He raised it, and it grew up with him and his children. It shared his food, drank from his cup and even slept in his arms. It was like a daughter to him.

'Now a traveller came to the rich man, but the rich man refrained from taking one of his own sheep or cattle to prepare a meal for the traveller who had come to him. Instead, he took the ewe lamb that belonged to the poor man and prepared it for the one who had come to him.'

David burned with anger against the man and said to Nathan, 'As surely as the Lord lives, the man who did this deserves to die! He must pay for that lamb four times over, because he did such a thing and had no pity.'

Then Nathan said to David, 'You are the man!'

Oasis

2 Samuel 12:13 - 14

Then David said to Nathan, 'I have sinned against the Lord.' Nathan replied, 'The Lord has taken away your sin. You are not going to die. But because by doing this you have made the enemies of the Lord show utter contempt, the son born to you will die.'

Imagine

David is king. He has a firm hold on his people. He no longer leads his troops personally but sends them out under trusted generals. The winter snow and the early rains have given way to sunshine. The crops have been sown and there's a feeling of expectation in the air.

It's evening. It's been a warm day and now the sun is beginning to set over the western edge of the city. Jerusalem - *the city of peace* - seems peaceful, even though out to the east over the River Jordan David's troops are confronting their enemies.

It's a lovely time of day. The light is softening, its midday glare gone, the sky gentling into pale blues and pinks. All over the city cooking fires are being lit, spreading a soft blue blanket of smoke just above the roofs of the single-storied houses. The city is waking up, stretching itself after the afternoon siesta, the shops opening up again for evening trade. Apart from the shopkeepers people are beginning to relax, the day's work coming to an end. Little groups of men meet on street corners, coalesce and drift apart.

This is the time when personal defences are down and tiredness loosens the awareness. David is watching the sunset, enjoying the view, thinking with some satisfaction, 'All this is mine.' The city, its people, the surrounding land. It's been a long hard road, but now he can take a quiet satisfaction in what he's achieved. He enjoys the feeling of success, the sense of power as he clenches then relaxes his hands.

Jerusalem is a small city crowded on a hill, its buildings jostling for space. From where David is standing he sees a jumble of flat rooftops. He looks down on them and watches the life around him. There's grain on some, stored from the last harvest, fuel stacked on others. There are beds and sleeping mats laid out, and a few children playing a game. Then another movement catches his eye. He looks down and sees a woman bathing. He looks away, then looks again. She is beautiful. David is human, male, his pulses quicken.

He turns away, trying to control his feelings. But he can't resist another look. He turns back and is lost. After all he is king. He thinks he deserves some reward for the hard years of struggle, the responsibilities that pile on him each day. And . . . well, he's only doing what so many do . . .

Market at Hebron

The woman was very beautiful, and David sent someone to find out about her. 2 Samuel 11:2 - 3

D avid began well as king. He *'reigned over all Israel, doing what was just and right for all his people.'* (2 Samuel 8:15). Then comes this incident which takes my breath away. So far in this saga David had been the hero, the wronged and persecuted man chosen by God to lead his people. He'd held fast to faith through times of great difficulty and deprivation, sometimes easily, sometimes with a desperation we can only imagine. Suddenly, in the days of success, David made a wrong choice. And it wasn't just a small mistake.

Wouldn't it have been better if the Bible had glossed over this relationship? It couldn't have been ignored entirely because later David and Bathsheba had another son, Solomon, but it could have been played down, sanitised. It might have been more comforting for later generations to see David as the perfect man of God, but the Bible's too honest for that.

And in the end, letting us see this less attractive side of David's character makes him more human. Like most other people, famous or not, he's a wounded personality blown about by his own emotions and in need of the grace and healing that only God can give. There's encouragement in that, reminding us that God works through imperfect, vulnerable human beings with all their failings. That's just as well; if he only worked through perfect people he wouldn't get much done because there aren't many of them around.

But how did this happen? This was the same David who'd faced Goliath, confident in God's strength; the same David who'd held on to faith through all his years in the desert. Perhaps in the increasing busyness of life, through the growing responsibilities of leading his people, David found less and less time for God. His faith was put into a smaller and smaller compartment of his life and became something 'I'll get back to when I have time'.

The longer this separation went on the easier it became to make the division more complete.

And from being central to life, faith becomes at best something for Sunday morning - or in David's case for the Sabbath - but irrelevant to 'real' life. David shut the door on God and felt free to act as he wished with no thought of the consequences, either to him or to anyone else.

I must admit, Lord,
that I find it satisfying
to see the great and good and mighty
bite the dust.
To see them vulnerable and weak
and plainly in the wrong.
And if I never rise
to stand on pedestals with them
at least it's possible
to pull them down to where I am.

And yet I feel a sadness too at David's plight.
That he should come to this.
Your man, so full of promise.
The one you chose and helped
and guided over all the years.
But now, his conscience callused over,
nerve endings dulled,
insensitive to all the pain
he gave to others,
the hurt done to himself,
he takes what isn't his.

A lesson there for all of us to learn.
(I put it in the plural, Lord,
so that the accusation
doesn't get too personal
and I can keep a modicum of comfort.)
The message is quite clear.
Temptation comes to all.
Sometimes full frontal
- please forgive the phrase -
more often silent and invisible in its subtlety,
creeping unrecognised into our lives.
My life. (On second thought
I'd better put it in the singular again,
the plural is too tempting
and let's me off the hook too easily.)
And maybe just because
I've never shared a bed
with other people's wives,
the pride that says that is itself a sin.
Lord, keep me from quick judgement
of other people's pain.

'Put Uriah in the front line where the fighting is fiercest.'
2 Samuel 11:15

With God firmly locked out of his life David sank deeper into trouble. His sensitivity as a poet and musician should have helped him imagine the pain and desolation his behaviour could bring to everyone involved. During David's time as a fugitive, Saul had given David's wife to another man. Had he forgotten the hurt he'd felt then? But David's rise to power had overlaid those feelings. He now had the power to do what he wished and that was all that mattered.

Bathsheba was pregnant. Unsuccessful in deceiving Uriah into sleeping with his wife so that he would believe the baby was his, David moved from adultery, through deception, to murder. Somehow he was able to justify it all to himself. After all it wouldn't be his hand that killed Uriah, so it wouldn't be his fault. And maybe David said to himself, 'Well, God can protect Uriah if he wants too.'

'Power corrupts,' says the wise man and we all agree, but in agreeing we look at other people rather than ourselves. We apply it to politicians and newspaper editors, and fat cats in industry, but it comes much nearer home than that.

We all hold power of some sort, and we all misuse it. There's power within the family; the unconscious manipulation of feelings. The influence of parents over children for good or bad. The mood swings to get one's own way, the quarrels or the silences when words can't persuade. And children too quickly learn ways of getting what they want.

There are, God forgive us, similar struggles within our church congregations, sometimes blatant, more often exercised in hidden ways, and often in the name of God. Even powerlessness can become an instrument to manipulate opinion and decision-making, and become power in its turn.

We're quick to justify it to ourselves at least. We use our power 'for the good of everyone'. Or so we say, and often with a shallow and bogus sincerity that insulates us from the truth. Yet, however much we turn our backs on God, however hard we lean on the door to keep him out of those dark and hidden corners, he's there waiting patiently. He may seem threatening at times, I'm sure David must have felt that, but he's waiting to restore, not condemn.

His presence isn't always gentle. He can create unease, put quiet questions into our minds, leave us uncomfortable and disturbed, but only to bring us back to himself. However much we may deny it, our hearts are restless until they find their rest in God, as Saint Augustine found.

One thing leads to another, Lord.
It's all so easy
having taken one small hesitant step
to take the next.
To tell myself
it doesn't really matter.
I'm not a murderer,
my sins are small
compared to some.
And I can take a quiet satisfaction
in claiming
that I am not as others are.
Until your voice reminds me
those were the words
the Pharisee spoke
to justify himself.

But as I pause for breath
before continuing my critical assessment
of just how weak I am,
proud, almost, of my own unworthiness,
I hear your voice again
reminding me of good.
Turning me to face the light
of your continuing presence
in my life.
Your grace a greater strength
than all the negatives I feel.

And gently, almost imperceptibly,
your healing starts its work
beneath the bruises'
of my self-inflicted hurt.
And I can face myself,
and you, again
in confidence that comes,
not from pretended strength
I know I don't possess,
but from the certainty
of your forgiveness
and the love that says
I can begin again.

The Lord sent Nathan to David.   2 Samuel 12:1

I wonder how Nathan knew the truth about David? His relationship with Bathsheba was obvious of course, since she'd moved into the palace and given birth to their son, but Nathan knew more than that.

Somehow he knew the truth of Uriah's death. Was it just through court gossip, the sort of rumour that would create banner headlines in the tabloid newspapers today? Was Nathan, an acute observer of human frailty, simply putting two and two together and finding the right answer? Or had he heard from Joab, the general who'd had to arrange the betrayal for the king? We might even see it as a revelation although, while not ruling that out, God seems to work more often through our human senses and abilities than in any other way. We simply don't know, and the mechanics of it don't matter as much as the truth behind it all.

What we do know is that nothing can be hidden for ever. For all his power and influence David couldn't keep his wrongdoing secret. In his heart he knew that what he'd done was wrong or he wouldn't have tried to keep it hidden. And even when secrets can for a time be hidden successfully from public view, they are still known to God.

Psalm 139 is a wonderful hymn to this truth:-

'Where can I go from your Spirit? Where can I flee from your presence?' sings the Psalmist. *'If I say, "Surely the darkness will hide me and the light become night around me," even the darkness will not be dark to you; the night will shine like the day, for darkness is as light to you.'*

In earlier days I used to find these words a bit threatening, implying that God was breathing down my neck, looking for the least little transgression, waiting to pounce. Now I see them differently. I rejoice in them because they tell me that God, who is love, is caring for me, overshadowing my every move, watching over me in sheer goodness. The threat becomes a comfort and a source of strength.

And if that seems to contradict what was happening in the confrontation between Nathan and David then we need to look ahead to the denouement. The confrontation was to make David face what he'd done and to bring him back to God, not to extend his punishment. And that's what he wills for each one of us.

Lord, as you dig
below the surface of my life,
removing the accumulated rubbish
of the years,
you bring into the light
so many buried things
I'd rather keep concealed.
The excavation's painful.
Layer after layer stripped back
to show what's underneath.
An archaeology of failure.

And bit by bit
as you unearth
all that lies buried
- no treasure trove -
my first reaction is to hide.
Burrow myself into the dark,
carve out a cave
and for a moment, mole like,
tell myself I'm safe from you.

But you, Lord,
gently relentless in pursuit,
persist in following me,
leaving nowhere to hide.
Your candle flame of truth
may flicker
but it lights my darkness
like the sun at dawn.
And as I'm brought reluctantly
into your light,
blinking, half-blinded
and still struggling,
I find that safety lies
not from but with you.

The pain I feel is therapeutic
and in your burning closeness
lies my healing.
Shine on me, Lord.

'You are the man!' 2 Samuel 12:7

I don't suppose anyone in the palace dared breathe the name of Uriah after Bathsheba had joined David there. We're not told how she got on with his other wives but life seems to have settled down. Until Nathan arrived. Nathan was welcomed by David. He thought well of prophets. It had been the prophet Samuel who had anointed him and supported him so long ago. Prophets were good, until now.

My imagination swings between two pictures of their confrontation. In the first, Nathan stands publicly before David and his whole court, telling his story about the rich man who used his power to steal the poor man's lamb. The story must have stirred powerful emotions in David, taking him back to his early life as a shepherd. A ewe lamb was something to be cared for in those days. Then, when David has committed himself, Nathan's denunciation rang out dramatically for all to hear.

In the second picture, I see David and Nathan in private, Nathan telling his story quietly and persuasively, and looking David in the eye with strong compassion as he faces him with the reality of his sin.

In either scenario the words must have been followed by a profound silence. David the warrior at war with himself as he tried to deal with the avalanche of emotions threatening to overwhelm him. Anger that anyone would dare question what he, the king, had done. Guilt making the anger stronger and hiding behind it. Fear at what this criticism might lead to. Embarrassment and shame to have it all brought out into the open.

I can almost feel David wishing for an instant that he had his spear in his hand to put an end to Nathan - before he remembered Saul and his spear all those years ago.

Something broke in David. His pride shattered, the armour he wore to shield himself from himself fell away, and he saw himself as Nathan saw him, as God saw him. It must have been a bleak moment of utter misery as David saw how far he'd fallen, how distant he was from that young man whose trust in God had been so complete. *'How are the mighty fallen'* - those words from David's elegy for Saul and Jonathan now applied to him.

I hear David whispering to Nathan, 'Is there a way back?' And that was the opportunity God had been waiting for. David unlocked the door and God stepped back into his life as God always will when he's given the invitation.

Someone said, 'When you open the door of your life to God, you find he's already opened the door of his life to you.'

Your truth is fire, Lord.
I think I know how David felt
as he heard
the words the prophet spoke.
Words straight from you.
No comfortable euphemisms
to dress them diplomatically
and make them easier to take.
Truth from the heart of truth itself.
It burns.

Now, while I stand,
a spectator
just watching from the sidelines,
the heat's not too intense.
And though my eyes may sting
in smoke from other people's flames,
I can maintain a distance
and a quiet satisfaction
at their discomfort.

But, Lord, your fire burns too close.
Singes the edges of my life,
then burns me to the core.
Your words are meant
as much for me as him.
There's nothing much to choose
between the two of us.
I've killed no sheep
but Lord I've taken
more than my fair share
of your goodwill.
That's pain enough.

But as I pause and gasp,
the wonder is
your love's a healing flame.
It leaves me scorched but whole.
Your balm may sting
but standing in the ashes
of my failures
I take a breath
and know
that I can start afresh.

Then David said to Nathan, 'I have sinned against the Lord.' Nathan replied, 'The Lord has taken away your sin. You are not going to die.'   2 Samuel 12:13

David made no excuses. He simply acknowledged the wrong he'd done. It's refreshing that he didn't try to blame the woman, Bathsheba. Many men do!

Nathan must have felt a moment of profound relief as he heard the words. He'd challenged the king. It was almost another David and Goliath incident, but this time with David transformed into the powerful villain and Nathan confronting him, armed only with the sling stones of God's truth.

This time though there was no killing. By the laws of the land, which the people believed had been given to them by God, David deserved to die. He'd broken at least three of the ten commandments - by coveting his neighbour's wife, then committing adultery, and finally by murdering her husband. He'd got in pretty deeply, and the penalty for both adultery and murder was death.

David came face to face with what he really was. His power was the facade behind which lived a compromised human being. I don't know when he sang the words we can read in Psalm 51, but they crystallise his feelings at this moment:-

> *'Have mercy on me, O God, according to your unfailing love;*
> *according to your great compassion blot out my transgressions . . .*
> *. . . For I know my transgressions, and my sin is always before me.'*

Then David experienced the wonder of forgiveness. 'The Lord has taken away your sin,' said Nathan. The immediacy takes the breath away. As he repents David sees the face of God's righteous judgement and finds it transformed instantaneously into the face of loving forgiveness.

There are times I find this aspect of God hard to accept. I'd prefer him to punish the sin, especially if it's been committed by someone else. After all that's what they deserve! But the grace of immediate forgiveness is hard to take. And even when I'm the sinner I sometimes feel I could face God a little more easily knowing that I'd paid for what I'd done, but that's not God's way.

His love overrides everything else. Jesus has shown us that.

Lord, is it really true?
The wonder of your love
just takes my breath away.
You leave me gasping.
It simply isn't reasonable to forgive
before exacting retribution.
It goes against the grain
of all the world holds dear.
Punishment should fit the crime,
and if it doesn't change the criminal
then double it.
Debts must be paid,
and when it's someone else
I find it very satisfying
to see them suffer for their sins.

And though it's not a party game,
I'd rather pay a forfeit
when it comes to you and me
so I could claim
I'd earned your favour
rather than take it as a gift.
I find forgiveness freely offered
a humbling experience
beyond anything I've known.
It hurts my pride.
I'd rather pay my way
and buy my round.

It's most unsettling, Lord,
to find that in the instant
that I face myself
and look away in shame
the slate's wiped clean.
Your love obliterates the debt
that stood between us -
although the debt was always my creation,
never yours -
and I'm restored.
Love beyond law and logic overwhelms me.
It can't be analysed,
its depth a mystery too deep to fathom.
I can do nothing but reach out
and hold it close.

'. . . the son born to you will die.' 2 Samuel 12:14

David may have been king but he was also a vulnerable human being. He'd been assured of God's forgiveness for the wrong he'd done but then his son fell ill and it felt as though God was punishing him. And how sad that this child of David and Bathsheba went into Biblical history with no name. As I stand alongside David and Bathsheba in my imagination and feel the helplessness and anguish as they watched their baby sicken and die, I have to ask the same question David must have asked. How could God's forgiveness be real when this was happening?

Guilt doesn't give up easily. It attacks the whole idea of forgiveness in whatever ways it can. What better way than to suggest to David that there was a link between his sin and the baby's suffering, but how wrong.

We need to take a firm hold on the assurances Jesus gives about the overwhelming love and forgiveness of God before we try to interpret incidents like this. Whose fault was it? Why did the child die? Nathan could only understand it as an act of God, a phrase we use so easily and usually wrongly. However much he tried to understand and link them, I'm sure the two events were separate. There was no cause and effect. I have to say honestly - if a little arrogantly - that I couldn't accept a God who would take the life of an innocent baby to punish the parent.

There are so many reasons for children's deaths. Some years ago my work took me to Bhutan, a small kingdom in the Himalayas. There were remote areas in the mountains where almost half the babies born died before they were five years old. This wasn't God's punishment but because the richer Western world hadn't got round to sharing modern medicine with them. Such things aren't caused by God's judgement but our inaction.

Blaming God may make it easier to fit things into the framework of our limited understanding but it doesn't make it true.

In his misery, and I'm sure Bathsheba must have felt the same even though her emotions aren't brought into the picture, David was living through another desert experience, another winter of bleak suffering. The good thing was that it threw him back on God. Again.

A friend of mine said that failure is a doorway to a new encounter with God, and that's what happened with David. He '. . . went into the house of the Lord and worshipped.' (v. 20). David took his turmoil and anguish, his mixed emotions, and offered them to God just as they were.

It may not have solved his problems immediately, but at least it reminded him, and reminds us, of another dimension to life.

I think I ask too many questions, Lord,
but that's the way I am.
My mind and my imagination
are your gifts to me,
gifts that I treasure
and find joy in using.
And if that means
I need more answers
than you're prepared to give,
I'm sorry,
but I'll go on asking questions anyway.

I wonder at the way
your world is organised.
The joys and sorrows,
highs and lows
and all the many happenings in between.
They seem so random,
hitting some and leaving others
apparently untouched.
And when it comes to suffering and death
the textbook answers never satisfy,
ring hollow, echo emptily,
and I am left
still knocking on a door
that never seems to open.

Perhaps I ask too much.
I'm sure I do,
and in the end
I know all I can do is trust.
That's what you ask.
That's why, I think,
your silence may be saying more to me
than all that words could say.
But still it's hard
and if I wait,
I wait impatiently
for that great moment when,
my doubts resolved,
my fears removed,
I stand before you
in the splendour of your presence.
No questions left.

Then David comforted his wife, Bathsheba . . . and she gave birth to a son, and they named him Solomon. The Lord loved him . . .   2 Samuel 12:24

God never gives up on people. Through all the drama of David's life God was there, working away on him. I was going to say 'like a potter with a lump of clay' but I'm not too comfortable with that image. Clay is inert. It's almost totally in the potter's control.

God has created us to be different. We have minds and wills and we can decide for ourselves how we use them and what we do with our lives. Whatever our circumstances there is always a choice. The alternatives may not be to our liking but there's usually more than one way to go.

David was no lump of clay. He was a powerful character with a strong will which helped him survive through turbulent events, even though it led him into deep trouble at times. He got on with life. He'd taken risks, faced difficulties, made decisions. At his best he was clearly conscious of God's presence. At his worst he could turn his back on God, but he never denied his existence, and was sensitive to his mistakes when they were pointed out to him.

And in Solomon's birth David's relationship with God was taken a step further. Solomon - the name has its origin in the word Shalom, *'peace'* - was also named Jedidiah, *'loved by the Lord'*. In Solomon God confirmed the future. He was the son who would consolidate all that David had accomplished, and who would build the Temple David had dreamed of. And an infinitely greater 'Son of David', Jesus, would seal all the purposes God had begun. But that would be much later.

God's purposes are rarely fulfilled instantaneously, although we think we'd like it better if they were. Often the wait is the hardest thing about our relationship with him, but he has his own timing. And he works patiently and slowly through us as he did through David.

His love and forgiveness outlive our restlessness and sin. That doesn't give us an excuse to trespass on his love without regard, it's not a licence to misbehave without thought of consequences, but it is the ultimate reality we cling to. *'Nothing,'* wrote Paul to Christians at Rome, *'nothing will be able to separate us from the love of God that is in Christ Jesus our Lord.'*

Time and again we may stumble as David did, but time and again we are lifted up by the same loving hands, restored to dignity and kinship as children of God.

Lord, when you spoke
of making highways straight,
of cutting down the gradients
on the hills,
and smoothing out rough places
perhaps I didn't understand.
My walk with you
seems different.
Sometimes I think
I'm travelling in circles
and after all my efforts
I'll be back where I began.

There are smooth roads at times,
I grant you that,
but generally they peter out
or lead to tracks
much rougher than I bargained for.
My breath comes short,
my knees are bruised and cut
from falling
in the rough and stumble
of my daily life.
The valleys I explore are deep
and though the beauty of the mountain beckons,
from where I stand
the climb's so steep.

Then looking back
along the path I've come
I realise
that the journey's not in vain.
Each footstep gained,
in ease or hardship,
brings me nearer to the goal.
And though the far horizon's
blue with mystery
and cloaked in haze,
I know I'm heading in the right direction.
Your presence gives encouragement
and strength to carry on
in certain knowledge
that my journey's end is you,
as its beginning.

. . . Israel's singer of songs.   2 Samuel 23:1

With the birth of Solomon David's life had reached its highest point. Israel had secure borders, a strong army and now an heir who would be king when David died. Perhaps this is the point at which we can leave him.

David could claim many titles. Poet, musician, warrior, king, but the best one was the last he was given, *'Israel's singer of songs'*. And what songs he sang. Songs full of the joy of God's presence; despair when God seemed to withdraw from him. Praise for deliverance from his enemies; impatience when God makes him wait. Anger when he sees the wicked flourish and the innocent suffer. Exultation in victory and wonder at the richness of God's mercy and forgiveness.

In some of his songs David sings of his own righteousness. In others he is deeply ashamed of his sinfulness. Often these conflicting thoughts are part of the same song, one emotion chasing the other, line by line.

Which is the real David? The saint or the sinner? The answer is both because, when the armour is removed, the roles played out and the real David emerges, we see him as a human being. A great man but flawed like the rest of us.

Writing a thousand years later, St. Paul confessed, *'I do not understand what I do. For what I want to do I do not do, but what I hate I do.'* (Romans 7:15). David would have agreed. Throughout his life David lived passionately and struggled with the chaos within, and the only difference between his life and ours is that his was played out on a larger, more dramatic stage. Although our lives are smaller the struggle's just the same.

All the music of human experience and emotion is in his singing, and David played out the harmonies and discords as he awaited the final movement that would lift him into the glory of the full presence of God, the song of his life ended, a new song ready to begin.

Waken my heart, Lord,
to the music of your love.
Help me to sing your song
as David did.
Sometimes he got it wrong
and so do I,
the notes all out of place,
the harmony destroyed.

And then
the melody grows faint,
eludes me altogether,
drowned in the discord
as my life wreaks havoc
with your harmonies.
And in the clash of will
I'm deafened by the silence,
not of your withdrawal,
but of mine.

Then in the loneliness,
the self-created emptiness,
your music comes again.
Your hand plays gently
on the taut strings of my life
offering me a chance
to sing again.

Fine tune me, Lord,
to hear the faintest note you play
and fit my life
around your melodies.
And help me
finally
to recognise
the tune I play is yours.
There all the time
if only I had listened.

Leprosy Mission contact addresses and telephone numbers

International Office:
The Leprosy Mission
80 Windmill Road
Brentford
Middlesex TW8 0QH
UK
Tel: 44 181 569 7292
Fax: 44 181 569 7808
e-mail: friends@tlmint.org
www.leprosymission.org/

TLM Trading Ltd. (for orders):
PO Box 212
Peterborough
PE2 5BR
Tel: 44 1733 239252
Fax: 44 1733 239258
e-mail: TLMTrading@dial.pipex.com

Africa Regional Office:
PO Box H G 893
Highlands
Harare
Zimbabwe
Tel: 263 4 733709
Fax: 263 4 721166
e-mail: tlmiaro@intellisoft.co.zw

Australia:
PO Box 293
Box Hill
Victoria 3128
Tel: 61 398900577
Fax: 61 398900550
e-mail: tlm.aust.nat@c031.aone.net.au

Belgium:
PO Box 20
1800 Vilvoorde
Tel/Fax: 32 22519983

Canada:
75 The Donway West, Suite 1410
North York
Ontario M3C 2E9
Tel: 1 416 4413618
Fax: 1 416 4410203
e-mail: tlm@tlmcanada.org

Denmark:
Skindergade 29 A, 1.,
1159 Copenhagen
Tel: 45 331 18642
Fax: 45 331 18645
e-mail: lepra@post3.tele.dk

England and Wales, Channel Islands & The Isle of Man:
Goldhay Way
Orton Goldhay
Peterborough PE2 5GZ
Tel: 44 1733 370505
Fax: 44 1733 370960
e-mail: post@tlmew.org.uk

Finland:
Hakolahdentie 32A4
00200 Helsinki
Tel: 358 9692 3690
Fax: 358 9692 4323

France:
BP 186
63204 Riom Cedex
Tel/Fax: 33 473 387660

Germany:
Kuferstrasse 12
73728 Esslingen
Tel: 49 711 353 072
Fax: 49 711 350 8412
e-mail: LEPRA-Mission@t-online.de

Hong Kong:
GPO Box 380
Central
Tel: 852 2805 6362
Fax: 852 2805 6397
e-mail: tlmhk@netvigator.com

Hungary:
Alagi Ter 13
Budapest 1151

India Regional Office:
CNI Bhavan
16 Pandit Pant Marg
New Delhi 110 001
Tel: 91 11 3716920
Fax: 91 11 3710803
e-mail: tlmindia@del2.vsnl.net.in

Italy:
Via Rismondo 10A
05100 Terni
Tel/Fax: 39 0744 811218
e-mail: arpe@seinet.it

Netherlands:
Postbus 902
7301 BD Apeldoorn
Tel: 31 553558535
Fax: 31 553554772
e-mail: leprazending.nl@inter.nl.net

New Zealand:
PO Box 10-227
Auckland 1004
Tel: 64 9 630 2818
Fax: 64 9 630 0784
e-mail: tlmnz@clear.net.nz

Northern Ireland:
Leprosy House
44 Ulsterville Avenue
Belfast BT9 7AQ
Tel: 44 1232 381937
Fax: 44 1232 381842
e-mail: 106125.167@compuserve.com

Norway:
c/o Bistandsnemnd
PO Box 2347 Solli
Arbingst. 11
0201 Oslo
Tel: 47 22438110
Fax: 47 22438730
e-mail: bistandn@online.no

Portugal:
Casa Adelina
Sítio do Poio
8500 Portimão
Tel: 351 82 471180
Fax: 351 82 471516
e-mail: coaa@telepac.pt

Republic of Ireland:
5 St James Terrace
Clonskeagh Road
Dublin 6
Tel/Fax: 353 126 98804
e-mail: 106125.365@compuserve.com

Scotland:
89 Barnton Street
Stirling FK8 1HJ
Tel: 44 1786 449266
Fax: 44 1786 449766
e-mail: lindatodd@compuserve.com

SEA Regional Office:
6001 Beach Road
#08-06 Golden Mile Tower
199589 Singapore
Tel: 65 294 0137
Fax: 65 294 7663
e-mail: pdsamson@tlmsea.com.sg

Southern Africa:
Private Bag X06
Lyndhurst 2106
Johannesburg
Tel: 27 11 440 6323
Fax: 27 11 440 6324
e-mail: Leprosy@infonet.co.za

Spain:
C/Beneficencia, 18 Bis-1º
28004 Madrid
Tel/Fax: 34 915945105
e-mail: mundosolidari@mx3.redestb.es

Sweden:
Box 145
692 23 Kumla
Tel: 46 19 583790
Fax: 46 19 583741
e-mail: lepra@algonet.se

Switzerland:
Chemin de Réchoz
1027 Lonay/VD
Tel: 41 21 8015081
Fax: 41 21 8031948

Zimbabwe:
PO Box BE200
Belvedere
Harare
Tel: 263 4 741817
e-mail: tlmzim@tlmzim.icon.co.zw

ALM International:
1 ALM Way
Greenville
S C 29601
U.S.A.
Tel: 1 864 537 7679
Fax: 1 864 271 7062
e-mail: amlep@leprosy.org